How To Sell
APARTMENT
BUILDINGS

How To Sell
APARTMENT
BUILDINGS
The Big Money
in Real Estate

Gary Earle

Longman Financial Services Publishing
a division of Longman Financial Services Institute, Inc.

While a great deal of care has been taken to provide accurate and current information, the ideas, suggestions, general principles and conclusions presented in this book are subject to local, state and federal laws and regulations, court cases and any revisions of same. The reader is thus urged to consult legal counsel regarding any points of law—this publication should not be used as a substitute for competent legal advice.

Executive Editor: Kathleen A. Welton
Development Editor: Joanne White
Copy Editor: Elizabeth Rubenstein
Cover Design: Salvatore Concialdi
Interior Design: Edwin Harris
Project Editor: Linda S. Miller

Published by Longman Financial Services Publishing
a division of Longman Financial Services Institute, Inc.

Printed in the United States of America.

88 89 90 10 9 8 7 6 5 4 3 2 1

Library of Congress Cataloging-in-Publication Data

Earle, Gary.
  How to sell apartment buildings.

  1. Apartment houses.   2. Real estate business.
I. Title.
HD1394.E24   1987   333.33'8   87-13964
ISBN 0-88462-716-0

*I dedicate this book to my wife, Carmen,
with whom I share my life and dreams and
whose faith, encouragement and inspiration
have made this book possible.*

ACKNOWLEDGMENTS

When John Donne said, "No man is an island," I am sure he intended to include each person who ever wrote a book.

Sharing the progress of this project with others has been a warm enriching experience for which I am deeply grateful.

I sincerely appreciate the interest, advice and assistance shown by professional associates and friends during the book's development. My sincere thanks to Dave Anderson, appraiser; Gilbert Barnes, title representative; George Corrigan, commercial real estate broker; Nancy Jeremiason, residential real estate broker; Michael F. La Gory, editor; Don Lang, certified public accountant; John Maggio, certified public accountant; Bernard M. Mann, attorney at law; Hershell T. Price, real estate investor and developer; Beth Sackett, residential real estate broker; Michael Vinti, senior loan officer, and Daniel M. Whitaker, real estate investor and developer.

I want to extend a special acknowledgment to Frank Freeman, whose creative talents made an invaluable contribution to the preparation of this book.

GARY EARLE

CONTENTS

The Starting Point

*"I have been poor and I have
been rich. Rich is better."*

—SOPHIE TUCKER

This book has a single purpose: to help you make more money
than you ever thought possible.

If that sounds like a bold promise, please accept it as such
because I am going to show you how to earn a six-figure income
year after year.

How? By selling apartment buildings.

All you need is a real estate license and a desire to be in a top-
income bracket, plus the special system explained in this book.

If you are not presently in real estate and are thinking of changing your career, you couldn't make a smarter move than to learn
how to sell apartment buildings.

Any good real estate school in your area can prepare you for
your licensing exam. In a few weeks, you can have your license
and get going! Meanwhile, you'll have learned my proven sales
techniques.

I know the system works because I developed it myself, and
I use it so successfully that I regard a $100,000 income as a sign
of a mediocre year.

I've also taught my method to others who have profited from
it. An agent with a large commercial brokerage firm was doing
so badly that he was about to be fired for being a poor producer.
In just his first year of using my system, his income jumped to
six figures.

My success began in 1975 when I was a 24-year-old graduate student in San Diego. I had a dream of cruising the South Pacific at the helm of my own sailboat, gliding from island to island in a Polynesian paradise. I impatiently wanted to make this treasured odyssey soon, instead of having to wait 40 years for retirement.

The dream quickly turned into a nightmare when I added up my assets, which consisted of a mortgaged VW Bug with a dented fender, four pieces of Salvation Army furniture and six boxes of college textbooks. To make things worse, employers were not standing in line to hire a guy with a liberal arts degree in political science.

My checking account balance was a miniature version of the national debt and my hotel waiter job was paying only five dollars an hour—including tips.

Meanwhile, back in my apartment (ironically, a symbol of my future career), I studied the problem and decided that I needed a job that would give me unlimited earning potential, flexible working hours and a chance to be my own boss.

Remembering that I had once sold more subscriptions to *Boys' Life* than anyone else in my Cub Scout pack, I decided on a sales career and, thinking big, I enrolled in real estate school.

In real estate school, of course, you can learn all about deeds, land contracts, joint tenancy, property law, what clothes to wear and other matters of greater or lesser importance. What you don't learn in real estate school is *how to make money*.

That's why you see so many neatly dressed real estate agents walking around with motivation speeches ringing in their heads and small change jingling in their pockets. Real estate school taught them how to make a passing grade on the license exam, but not how to make sales.

I decided that selling houses was not for me—too much work, time and frustration with too small a return to meet my ambitious needs.

Then the idea struck like lightning. On my way home from real estate class, I stopped for a red light and there it was across the street—a row of large apartment buildings.

I could almost feel the ocean spray on my face as my boat cut through the shimmering Pacific waves! The dream was back.

It was pure simple logic. Someone owned those buildings. Someday, maybe today those properties would be for sale and someone would buy them. And, most important to me, someone would make one terrific commission. I couldn't think of a more deserving candidate for those big dollars than me. All I needed was to learn how to market apartment buildings.

That's where I was stopped by the stone wall of reality. I searched every source I could think of—libraries, bookstores, publishers' lists, real estate schools, commercial brokerage firms, banks, real estate information agencies and other likely places. I came up empty. Not a single book, course or set of guidelines was specifically devoted to selling apartment buildings.

The only answer was to create my own approach to marketing apartments, to organize a basic system, test it, refine it and put it into a form that could be used to sell any apartment building in any area.

The method worked.

In just three years, starting with nothing, I earned enough in commissions to buy a 52-foot sailboat and support myself, without working, during a two-year cruise to Hawaii, French Polynesia and other enchanted isles in the South Pacific.

When I returned to San Diego in 1982, I sold my boat and looked forward to the opportunity of selling apartments again. However, my former clients were no longer on my roster and I had to start from scratch again. To make things worse, the real estate market was in the depths of the worst recession the nation had seen since the 1930s.

Then, something amazing happened.

Using the techniques described in this book, I began to sell apartments almost immediately. During my first year back in the business, my income was once more in six figures.

At this point, I can hear someone asking, "Why apartment buildings? Why not sell multimillion dollar office complexes, industrial parks and shopping centers?"

Again, the answer is a matter of plain logic. There are more apartment buildings than all the office highrises, industrial properties and shopping centers combined.

Apartments are also easy for most investors to understand, rent and manage. And because apartment buildings come in all sizes—from two units to several hundred units—buyers have a wide range of choices to suit their available capital and their income needs.

Another major reason to concentrate on apartment buildings is the durable value of these properties. In any real estate cycle, apartment buildings are some of the first investment properties to go up in value and among the last to come down. The reason is solid reality. Regardless of business conditions, everyone needs a place to live. And with single-family homes priced increasingly beyond the reach of most wage earners, apartments offer the only affordable housing alternative.

Now, some news that may surprise you.

In spite of the huge earnings to be made selling apartment buildings, only a small handful of brokers, agents and investors are walking away with the biggest share of the money.

Why? Because most people do not know how to deal with the apartment market. Specifically, they don't know the *system* for selling apartments.

But *you* will learn this system because you are reading this book, the first definitive guide of its kind.

Again, I hear a question: "Do I need a certain talent to be successful at selling apartment buildings?"

The answer is an emphatic no. Selling apartment properties is a matter of *method*, not a gift of the gods. In fact, an ivory tower, genius type could actually fail because the system you are about to learn is so sensible and practical.

All you have to do is use the method, step-by-step, and stay with it. Also, you do not need to be a workaholic. I don't like working nights, weekends or holidays, and with my system I don't have to. Regular well-spent workweeks will bring you the rewards you want. Your earnings are limited only by the degree of energy you're willing to put into your new career.

A real estate license can be either a wall decoration or a ticket to a steady high income. Selling apartment buildings is a numbers game, and I'm going to show you how to win.

GARY EARLE

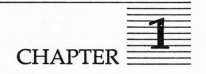
Sizing Up the Market

*"There is only one success—to
be able to spend your life in your
own way."*

—CHRISTOPHER MORLEY

If you read at an average speed, in as little as three or four hours you'll know how to begin reaching two of the greatest goals you could ever set for yourself. One is a lucrative career selling apartment buildings, a field with virtually unlimited income potential. The other achievement, related to the first, is a wonderful new personal life, enriched by a degree of independence and confidence you may never have experienced before. Above all, you'll be in control of your time, with the freedom to do and have the things you've always wanted.

At this point, I actually hope you are skeptical.

If that sounds like a strange statement from someone who is going to show you how to make considerable money, remember that knowing *why* opportunities exist is as important as learning *how* to take advantage of them.

The more clearly you see the potential in the apartment market, the better you can visualize your place in the picture. Therefore, I welcome your show-me attitude at the start because it demonstrates that you're an individual who demands facts, figures and proof—exactly the kind of person who is ideally suited for selling apartment buildings. Let's begin with basic marketplace realities.

First, there are two sources of commissions for you: the sale of new apartment buildings and the resale of existing ones. Second—and unlike most businesses that produce good incomes only when the economy is flourishing—selling apartments can deliver frequent sizable commissions whether the real estate market is moving up or down.

How big is the market? Look at these spectacular facts:

In just four years, from 1982 through 1985, 1.5 million new apartment units were built in the United States. These properties have a market value of approximately $45 *billion*. That immense figure far exceeds the gross national product produced by many countries.

Furthermore, the rising volume of building permits issued indicates that this strong multifamily construction trend will continue. The expanding apartment building activity represents an enormous opportunity for apartment salespeople (including *you*), because apartment developers usually prefer to sell their new projects to investors, rather than to retain and manage the complexes themselves.

Sales of existing apartments also are moving ahead at a record pace in almost every area of the country. Therefore, no matter where you live, commissions on resales are at your fingertips.

Investors, both individuals and syndicates, are ready prospects for buying apartment properties, which are widely recognized as some of the most valuable real estate commodities in the entire economy. In San Diego County alone, almost 30,000 apartment units worth an estimated $1.2 billion changed hands in 1985. The rest of the California market has been just as hot, with strong sales in the San Francisco Bay area, Los Angeles and Orange County. Turnover continued at a fast pace in 1986 as well, despite impending tax reform. In Phoenix almost 24,000 apartment units were sold in 1985, with similarly heavy trading action in other parts of the Sun Belt in the southwestern United States. In the South, Atlanta reported 25,000 apartment units sold in 1985.

Brisk apartment building sales were reported for Portland and other cities in the Pacific Northwest, with $250 million in apartments sold in Seattle alone.

In the same year, even economically depressed areas saw energetic apartment building sales. In Houston, for instance, 53,000 units were sold, despite slow activity in other sectors.

Think of all those real estate commissions waiting to be earned by people who know how to sell apartment buildings! And those opportunities exist in all parts of the country.

The Midwest, Chicago, Indianapolis and St. Paul all produced large volumes of apartment building sales. As an example of the continuous sales action, there was an ownership turn-over of approximately one-third of the apartment units in Kansas City in just four years (between 1982 and 1986).

In some extremely active markets with rapidly escalating prices, apartments not only sell well, but the same complexes often change hands more than once in a short period of time. More sales, more commissions!

If you need more convincing about the opportunities available to you, consider this: to maximize their return on investment and tax benefits, most apartment owners sell their buildings every five to six years. That fact means that approximately 17 percent to 20 percent of all apartment buildings are sold every year.

Meanwhile, the demand for apartment buildings keeps growing. More and more people are turning to apartment housing because rising prices are shutting them out of the home-buying market. Also, the increasing number of single-person and two-member households strengthens the demand for apartment living. Presently, no signs point to this trend changing.

The result is that in many parts of the country, new apartment construction lags behind demand, causing low vacancy rates, higher rents and rising appreciation of apartment properties. With these factors working for you, you need only match the right property with the right buyer. Therefore, you can look forward to a solid secure future as an apartment sales specialist.

You should no longer need much imagination to picture the huge income available to you. However, you must perform one task—and the sooner the better: do some mental housecleaning. Dust off your dreams about making big money. Those bright happy visions you once had can now become real. Scrap any ideas about settling for a mediocre income. Toss out thoughts about limitations and stop being hampered by a job you don't like.

That's all in the past. From this minute on, you're going to think big money because you now know how much is out there waiting for you. And you're going to succeed.

SUMMING UP WHAT YOU'VE LEARNED
IN CHAPTER 1

The apartment building sales market is one of the largest of all areas of commercial real estate activity. Keep these facts in mind as you look at a new future for yourself as an apartment sales specialist.

1. Unlike most businesses that provide good incomes only when the economy is flourishing, selling apartment buildings can give you frequent sizable commissions whether the market is up or down.

2. In just four years, from 1982 through 1985, 1.5 million new apartment units were built in the United States. Their market value—about $45 *billion*—exceeds the gross national product of many *entire nations*.

3. Most apartment building owners sell their properties every five to six years. Approximately 17 percent to 20 percent of all apartment buildings are sold each year. Repeat sales can mean repeat commissions for *you*.

4. In many markets apartments not only sell well, they are marketed with continuously escalating prices. Higher prices, bigger commissions!

5. Demand for apartment buildings keeps growing as more and more people find apartment living the only alternative to high-priced home ownership.

6. You have *two* vast sources of commissions: sales of new apartment buildings and resales of existing ones.

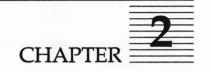

Gaining Market Knowledge

*"The beginning is the important
part of the work."*

—PLATO

The bucks start here.

I said earlier that this is a numbers game. It truly is. And, like mastering any game, you must first learn the basics in order to play and win. In selling apartments, as in all sales activities, this means learning all that you can about the product you want to sell and the marketplace in which you want to sell it.

Three components form the basic structure for successful apartment sales.

1. rental market information
2. comparable sales data
3. financing facts

All of these "building blocks" fit together to help you gain the fundamental market knowledge you need to start your career. The more you know about this trio of elements the better you'll be able to construct sales with my proven techniques.

Pay close attention because everything you'll learn on the following pages will have a direct bearing on how apartment buildings are priced for sale, the subject of the next chapter.

MAKING A RENTAL SURVEY

This is square one. Since apartment buildings derive their value from their ability to generate income, you must begin your new career in apartment sales by learning rental values in your marketplace. You gain this knowledge by conducting a rental survey. The main objectives of your rental survey will be to determine:

1. the rental prices of various types of apartment units (that is, what is the cost of a one-, two- or three-bedroom apartment?).
2. what effect amenities, such as pools, tennis courts, covered parking and so on have on the value of those rents.
3. how building size, age, condition and quality affect rental value.
4. how high vacancy rates are. (I'll explain how to determine vacancy rates later in the chapter.)

First you must stake out your territory, selecting those geographical areas in which you want to concentrate most of your efforts. This step is especially important if you live in a large metropolitan area because you can effectively cover more ground in less time if you work within a certain part of the city.

Another reason for zeroing in on a particular region is that it is easier to become an expert in a well-defined area than it is to become knowledgeable about a whole galaxy of apartments scattered all over the map.

Your reputation as a skilled professional is like money in the bank. When buyers and sellers know that you have the information they need, sales doors will open for you. The best way to reach expert status is to thoroughly understand a specific apartment area. Then, as time goes on, acquaint yourself with additional neighborhoods. I can assure you that your territory will rapidly expand. I began my apartment sales career specializing in a small San Diego coastal neighborhood with a few hundred apartment buildings in it. In less than two years I was working the entire county containing thousands of buildings.

You probably already know where the apartment neighborhoods are located in your city. If so, you're ready to define your territory and start making your rental survey. A good place to begin would be in an area with which you are familiar (a neighborhood near your home or real estate office, for instance, provided that numerous apartment buildings stand in those locations).

If no apartments are situated near you or you don't know their locations elsewhere in your city, many sources of information are available to you.

Most cities have zoning laws restricting apartment development to certain areas. Generally, where you find one apartment building, you'll find many others. You can obtain a map from the city zoning office that will show you the apartment areas in your locale.

Another place to look is title insurance companies. In many parts of the country they maintain large customer service departments that can provide you with abundant information concerning the locations of apartment buildings.

A good chance also exists that your local chamber of commerce has published an apartment guide for new renters coming into the community. This type of guide normally lists the areas throughout the city where rental housing can be found.

Once you've defined your territory, you can start gathering some of the information for your rental survey before you even leave home. Pick up your newspaper, especially the Sunday edition, and turn to the classified ad section. You'll need much more detailed information than you'll find in your newspaper, but by studying the "Apartments for Rent" columns, you can gain a broad overview of what is happening in the apartment market in which you've chosen to work.

To obtain specific data, you'll need to go out into the field and do some investigative work. After just a few days of talking with on-site apartment managers, you'll have the answers to the key questions that we noted earlier. The rental survey form shown in Figure 2–1 will make your job much easier. The form is virtually self-explanatory, but let's take a minute to go over some items.

In the categories for outdoor amenities and apartment features, mark yes or no after each item, depending on whether the complex offers them. After utilities, note whether the owner or the tenant pays the gas and electricity bills. Normally, the owner will provide water. However, if the tenants pay their own water bills, note that too.

In the number of units and apartment type columns list the unit mix, that is, how many one-, two- or three-bedroom apartments are in the building. Under square footage, mark the size of the apartments of each type. If you can't obtain the exact meas-

FIGURE 2–1   Rental Survey Form

Building Address _____

Building Name _____

Number of Units _____ Manager's Name _____

Date of Survey _____ Manager's Phone _____

Property Information

No. of Bldgs. _____ No. of Stories _____ Condition _____

Age _____ Type of Construction _____

No. Covered Parking Spaces _____ No. Uncovered Parking Spaces _____

Total No. of Parking Spaces _____

Outdoor Amenities

Pool(s) _____ Jacuzzi _____ Sauna _____ Rec. Room _____

Tennis Courts _____ Other Rec. Amenities _____

Apartment Features

Range & Oven _____ Refrigerator _____ Dishwasher _____

Patios/Balconies _____ Air Cond. _____ Carpets _____

Drapes _____ Disposals _____ Utilities _____

Other Features _____

Rental Information

No. of Units	Apt. Type	Sq. Ft.	Mo./Rent	Rent/Sq.Ft.
_____	_____	_____	_____	_____
_____	_____	_____	_____	_____
_____	_____	_____	_____	_____

Deposit Policy _____

Restrictions _____

Occupancy

Tenant Type _____

Total No. of Units _____ No. of Units Vacant _____

Vacancy Rate _____

Additional Comments _____

_____

urement, an approximation will do at this stage. Rent per square foot is determined by dividing the monthly rent by the apartment's square footage. A 650-square-foot one-bedroom apartment at $400 per month rents for $.62 per square foot ($400/650 = $.62). This information will give you a common denominator with which to compare the rental rates of apartments of differing size.

The vacancy rate is found by dividing the number of vacant units by the total number of apartments in the complex. A ten-unit apartment building with one vacancy has a ten-percent vacancy rate (1/10 = 10 percent). However, a more accurate picture of the vacancy rate in your territory can be ascertained after you have completed your survey. Add the total number of vacancies in all the buildings you have surveyed and divide the sum by the total number of units. For example, if you have discovered 68 vacancies in a total of 850 apartment units, the vacancy rate for your territory would average eight percent (68/850 = 8 percent).

Remember, you're developing a market profile of apartment buildings in your *entire territory*. Later, when you begin to price apartment complexes, the figures you are gathering in your rental survey will serve as a measuring stick to gauge whether a specific building is above or below average in vacancies, rent levels and other factors. You're piecing together a complete picture of the market by compiling facts and figures about a sizable number of buildings.

Fill out the form as completely as possible. Once you know the particulars on any given building, you'll have a valuable reference source for use throughout your sales career. However, because market conditions change, it's a good idea to update your rental survey information every 6 to 12 months by calling the resident manager. You won't have to start from scratch, but you will definitely want to know any new facts on rental rates, vacancy rates and amenities that may have been added to the apartment property. Staying up to date on rental surveys makes you look and feel like a real professional.

To begin your rental survey you need a supply of blank survey forms. (Type the format of the rental survey form in Figure 2–1 and reproduce it on an office copy machine.) To make additional notes on the property you are visiting, take along a few blank sheets of paper the same size as the rental survey form (to avoid scribbling on the form itself).

Now drive out into the territory you have selected, park your car on a side street and begin walking the neighborhood.

You'll want to survey a representative sample of the types of buildings that exist in your territory. These should include both smaller and larger apartment complexes as well as buildings of varying quality. The idea is to get a valid cross section of apartment properties so that you will have a realistic profile of the buildings in your area.

While it's hard to say exactly how many buildings you should survey, 15 to 20 properties spread throughout your territory should be the minimum. In any event, keep surveying until you feel you are totally on top of rental values in your chosen area.

Now let's start asking questions and gathering data.

After you've knocked on the apartment manager's door, you can approach him or her in two good ways. The first is the direct route. Simply tell the manager that you're a real estate agent specializing in the sale of apartment properties in the area and that you are conducting a rental survey. Hand him or her your business card and ask if you can pose some questions regarding the complex. I'd be surprised if you're ever turned down.

I always receive excellent cooperation from resident managers when I use this method, particularly because I offer to share with them the information I have collected on other buildings. Since one of the resident manager's primary duties is to stay abreast of rental rates in the area, this information can be of great value to him or her.

However, at times you may want to use a more subtle approach, especially if you know or sense that the resident manager might feel insecure about the building undergoing a possibe change of ownership. Here you can pose as a prospective tenant. As a potential renter, you should be able to inspect any vacant apartments and have a chance to ask enough questions of the manager to complete your rental survey. However, you'll have to develop a ''cover story'' so that you can answer—with some conviction—any questions directed to you by the manager. You'll also have to remember all the information you've gathered until you can return to your car and fill out your survey form.

To continue, assuming you have introduced yourself as an apartment marketing specialist, complete the survey form as shown in Figure 2-2. Then ask if you can see any of the vacant

FIGURE 2–2 Completed Rental Survey Form

Building Address __3250 DIAMOND ST.__

Building Name __PLAZA DEL SOL APARTMENTS__

Number of Units __18__ Manager's Name __RICHARD AUSTEN__

Date of Survey __OCT., 1986__ Manager's Phone __485-6923__

Property Information

No. of Bldgs. __2__ No. of Stories __2__ Condition __EXCELLENT__

Age __10 YRS.__ Type of Construction __WOOD FRAME/STUCCO__

No. Covered Parking Spaces __0__ No. Uncovered Parking Spaces __22__

Total No. of Parking Spaces __22__

Outdoor Amenities

Pool(s) __YES-1__ Jacuzzi __NO__ Sauna __NO__ Rec. Room __NO__

Tennis Courts __NO__ Other Rec. Amenities __OUTDOOR BAR-B-QUE AREA__

Apartment Features

Range & Oven __YES__ Refrigerator __YES__ Dishwasher __2 AND 3 BR's ONLY__

Patios/Balconies __YES__ Air Cond. __NO__ Carpets __YES__

Drapes __YES__ Disposals __YES__ Utilities __TENANTS PAY GAS & ELEC.__

Other Features __UNITS ON WEST SIDE HAVE CANYON VIEWS.__

Rental Information

No. of Units	Apt. Type	Sq. Ft.	Mo./Rent	Rent/Sq.Ft.
10	1BR/1BA	650	$410	$.63
4	2BR/2BA	900	$525	$.58
4	3BR/1½BA	1050	$595	$.57

Deposit Policy __$300 DEPOSIT ON 1 AND 2 BR'S, $400 ON 3 BR'S.__

Restrictions __NO PETS__

Occupancy

Tenant Type __MOSTLY ADULT, SOME CHILDREN IN 3 BR. UNITS.__

Total No. of Units __18__ No. of Units Vacant __1__

Vacancy Rate __5.5%__

Additional Comments

__PRIDE OF OWNERSHIP COMPLEX, NICELY LANDSCAPED COURTYARD__

apartments. By touring some empty units you can get an idea of the quality and size of various types of apartments.

In making my rental surveys, I ask additional questions of the manager to further enhance my feel for what is happening to rental rates in the area. I always ask the manager if he or she thinks the rents at his or her building are above, below or at market levels. Again, what you're trying to do is figure out where the rental rates should be. I also ask if the apartments are hard to rent. Do they stay vacant long? How much potential renter traffic comes through the building? The answers to the last two questions can help you determine how high the demand level is for rental units in the area.

Last, but not least important, I ask if the manager knows whether the owner has any interest in selling the building and how I might contact him or her. (How to locate apartment building owners will be discussed in more detail in Chapter 6.)

Here are some valuable tips to help you analyze your data once you've completed surveying your territory.

1. After you've surveyed the requisite number of buildings, you should have a pretty clear view of what owners are charging for various types of apartments. However, the rent that owners are receiving may or may not accurately reflect what the market will bear.

2. A vacancy rate of five percent to eight percent is considered a healthy level for both tenants and landlords. At this level the law of supply and demand will generally be in balance. Landlords should be able to increase rents modestly every year, but not at a rate that will put an undue burden on tenants. If vacancy rates in your territory are in the five percent to eight percent range, you can comfortably conclude that the average asking rents your survey has revealed are, in fact, *market* rents.

3. When vacancy rates dip below five percent the increased demand and reduced supply will allow rental rates to rise at a sharper pace. However, it can take some time for this information to spread throughout the marketplace and landlords may not have recognized the opportunity to raise rents. Therefore, if your survey shows vacancy rates under five percent you can conclude that market forces will permit rental rates higher than those asked by landlords.

4. Conversely, as vacancy rates approach or surpass ten percent, excess supply will spur price competition among landlords and rents will stabilize or even decrease. When this is the case, you might conclude that market rents are below asking rents.

One last thing before we move on to the next topic.

Be sure to take a camera with you when you make your rental survey. Shoot a picture of each apartment complex you visit, taking care to include the identification sign (usually in front of the building) and the street address. This photo will not only help you visually recall the building you inspected, but it will also be part of an important selling technique that will be discussed in Chapters 6 and 7.

COMPARABLE SALES DATA

Square two in your quest for market knowledge consists of compiling information about the recent sales of apartment properties in your territory. This is what is known in the real estate vernacular as finding *comparable sales data*. The facts and figures you collect about these sales will provide a basis of comparison to help you determine the value of other apartment buildings.

The information you need about a recently sold property is quite basic. You'll want to know the following:

1. address of the property
2. number of apartment units in the building and the unit mix (The unit mix is the number of studio, one-, two- or three-bedroom apartments that the building contains.)
3. date of the sale
4. names of the buyer and seller
5. selling price
6. terms of the sale (How much cash did the seller use for the down payment and what were the financing arrangements?)
7. square footage of the units and the total rentable square footage of the complex
8. apartment rental rates at the time of sale
9. age and condition of the complex at time of sale
10. names of any real estate brokers involved in the sale

You can obtain comparable sales data from many sources. The easiest and quickest, however, is from companies that specialize in compiling this data for sale to the real estate industry. One of the largest sources of this information is Real Estate Data, Inc., a company that gathers and disseminates apartment data on 300 key markets in 48 states. The company supplies subscribers with apartment sales data, updated monthly; (this data is on microfiche cards. You can obtain full details on this service by contacting Real Estate Data, Inc., 2398 Northwest 119th Street, Miami, FL 33167. The toll-free phone number is 1-800-327-1085.

Many regional and local companies also provide comparable sales data. Figures 2–3 and 2–4 are excellent examples of such information as provided in Arizona and California by Comps Incorporated. The sales data can be obtained monthly by subscription or on an individual need basis. You can reach Comps Incorporated by calling 619-457-2274 in California and 602-952-9911 in Arizona.

Be sure to search too in the multiple listing service of your local board of realtors. It can always be a prime source of comparable sales data.

Inquire within your real estate community to find out what other comparable sales data services might be available to you.

If, for some reason, a service of this type is not offered in your area, or you don't want to incur the expense of a subscription, you can compile the information yourself.

As I mentioned earlier, title insurance companies can be a valuable source of apartment information. Since their business is insuring title to a property upon sale, they maintain vast records of all sales transactions in a given county. Depending on practices in your area, title companies may provide information on these sales as a free service in the hope you will recommend your clients to them.

Real estate appraisers are also an excellent source of comparable sales data. Generally, a strong flow of information passes between brokers and real estate appraisers concerning the details of sales transactions. Look in the yellow pages of your telephone directory for appraisers in your area and give them a call. They should be more than happy to share with you any details about sales with which they are familiar because soon you'll be completing sales of your own and you'll be able to return the favor.

FIGURE 2–3

COMPS INCORPORATED   9605 Scranton Rd., 7th Floor San Diego, CA 92121

LNA-3629-01-87
5: Northridge/Granada Hills
$1,353,000(c)   56-D/3

[619] 457-2274

APARTMENT

36 UNIT APARTMENT BUILDING
• • • • • • • • • • • • •
984 Peach Avenue
Los Angeles, CA 91345

BUYER: (213)660-5000

John S. Rogers
2444 Camino Del Rio North
Los Angeles, CA 90022

SELLER: (213)663-6600

Peach Ave. Apartments, Ltd.
c/o Charles L. Spalding
3518 1st Ave., Ste 410
Sherman Oaks, CA 91436

INCOME DATA:

PROJ ANN GROSS INCOME	$	174,240
Equates to $.54/sf/mo		
Less: 3% vacancy	<$	5,227>
PROJ GROSS OPER INCOME	$	169,013
Less: Estimated Expenses		
(32% or $2.07/sf/yr)	<$	55,757>
EST NET ANNUAL INCOME	$	113,256

See Reverse

LOAN DATA:

TD/LENDER/BALANCE   ANN PMT
1st TD World S&L $947,000 $ 95,554
  (VIR) 9.5% 30 yr amtz

EST NET ANNUAL SPENDABLE $ 17,702

VITAL DATA:

Closng date: August 11, 1986
Document # : 399895
Sale price : $1,353,000(c)
Down paymnt: $406,000/30%
Est net inc: $113,256
Cap rate   : 8.4%
Spendable : $17,702
Spend. rate: 4.4%
Bldg sq ft : 27,000(APX)
Price/sq ft: $50.11
Price/unit : $37,583
Gross mult : 7.8
Studios   : 0/0%
1 bedroom : 24/67% (1+1)
2 bedroom : 12/33% (2+2)
3 bedroom : 0/0%
Other   : 0/0%
Prk:sp/unit: 48:1.3
Acres:d.u./: 1.15 : 31.3
Zoning   : R3, Los Angeles
Age (yrs) : 15
Imprv ratio: 78%
Trade   : No

LISTING:
(213)650-1333
Commercial Real Estate Co
2700 Waring Dr., Ste 214
Los Angeles, CA 90023
Steven Hing

BROKERAGE

SELLING:
(818)743-8100
Valley Investment Prop.
1480 12th St., Ste 425
Encino, CA 91316
Kevin Anderson

FIGURE 2–4

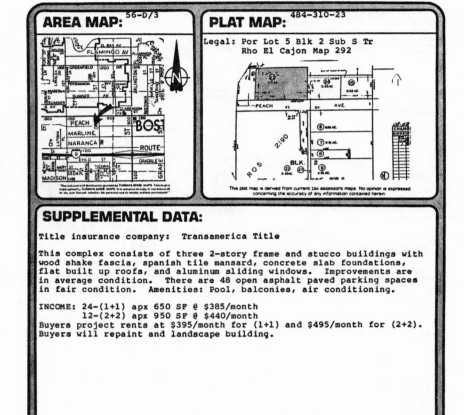

AREA MAP: 56-D/3

PLAT MAP: 484-310-23

Legal: Por Lot 5 Blk 2 Sub S Tr
Rho El Cajon Map 292

This plat map is derived from current tax assessors maps. No opinion is expressed concerning the accuracy of any information contained herein.

SUPPLEMENTAL DATA:

Title insurance company: Transamerica Title

This complex consists of three 2-story frame and stucco buildings with wood shake fascia, spanish tile mansard, concrete slab foundations, flat built up roofs, and aluminum sliding windows. Improvements are in average condition. There are 48 open asphalt paved parking spaces in fair condition. Amenities: Pool, balconies, air conditioning.

INCOME: 24-(1+1) apx 650 SF @ $385/month
        12-(2+2) apx 950 SF @ $440/month
Buyers project rents at $395/month for (1+1) and $495/month for (2+2).
Buyers will repaint and landscape building.

SOURCE: Reprinted with permission from COMPS Incorporated.

As your business grows, so will your contacts with other apartment brokers and you'll probably be exchanging information about the details of each other's sales. In fact, from time to time, you and another broker may be cooperating on the same transaction. For reasons of mutual benefit, it's worthwhile to become acquainted with other people involved in selling apartment buildings.

Another way to collect comparables is to visit the offices of the county recorder or keeper of public records. All changes of title are recorded by the county in which the property is located. You can obtain the names of the buyer and seller from the recorded grant deed and call those parties to get additional information about the sale. The staff in the county offices also may be able to show you other ways to use their filed information on past sales. For instance, most states charge a transfer tax when a property changes hands. The recorder can tell you how much tax was paid on a given transfer and the formula used to compute the tax. With this information, you can work the numbers backward to arrive at the sale price.

Make sure, too, that you read the real estate sections of your local newspapers, especially those papers that concentrate on reporting local business activity. Such publications often report sales of properties on a weekly or even daily basis. These reports normally list the names of the buyer and seller, together with the names of any real estate brokers involved. Again, you can contact the parties and get the data you require.

Most likely, no single source will provide you with all the information you want. But with a little investigative zeal, you should be able to piece together all the facts you need to know about a particular sale. After a bit of practice, you'll find that tracking down information is as easy as pressing the buttons on your phone. Best of all, playing sleuth pays off in faster sales action for you.

FINANCING FACTS

Since few investors purchase properties entirely with their own cash, keeping up-to-date on the financing market is of paramount importance to you. Money is a commodity and, like any commodity, its price varies in the marketplace. Investors often rely on their real estate agents to advise them of the current costs of borrowing money and to tell them how to structure the most advantageous financing for a sale or purchase. Since we will take an in-depth look at apartment building financing in Chapter 4, the following will serve as a brief introduction.

Types of Financing

There are two types of financing normally involved in an apartment sale. The first, conventional financing, consists of loans obtained from institutional sources such as banks, savings and loan associations and insurance companies. These sources offer an array of fixed and variable rate loans, and securing information about these loans is easy. Simply contact the various lending institutions in your area and ask their real estate loan officers to explain to you the different lending programs they offer. You'll find these people most cooperative because they will recognize you as a potential source of loan business for them.

The second form of financing is that which sellers of a property carry back themselves. Seller financing is nothing new to real estate, but it really came into vogue during the high-interest rate, tight money market of the early 1980s under the banner of "creative financing." The major example of this kind of financing is sellers carrying back second or third mortgages. As with conventional financing, rates and terms of seller financing fluctuate with market forces. Investigating the terms of seller financing while you collect your comparable sales data will tell you prevailing rates for this method of funding transactions. Besides learning current interest rates, you will also want to know the length of time that sellers are willing to carry the financing.

By now, you have acquired a basic awareness of how the apartment market works. You have learned how to take a rental survey, gather comparable sales data and find financing information. With a little practice, you'll be amazed and pleased by how quickly you'll gain a large amount of valuable market knowledge.

Let's start putting that knowledge to work in pricing apartments, the subject of the next chapter.

SUMMING UP WHAT YOU'VE LEARNED
IN CHAPTER 2

Gaining an accurate knowledge of your market is essential to building a career in apartment property sales. Remember the following points:

1. Rental market information and comparable sales data are the key elements in analyzing your local area.

2. Select a territory in which you want to concentrate most of your sales activities.

3. Use the rental survey form shown in this chapter to make a comprehensive profile of each apartment building you visit.

4. Survey a minimum of 15 to 20 apartment properties in your selected territory.

5. Get the data you need from the resident manager, who can often provide additional information on tenants, vacancies and the neighborhood.

6. A vacancy rate of five percent to eight percent is considered healthy for tenants and landlords. As vacancy rates dip below this level, rental rates will escalate at a sharper pace. Vacancy rates of ten percent and more may indicate that rental prices are too high.

7. Gathering comparable sales data shows what similar apartment buildings are selling for in your area. When reviewing sales data, make sure you compare ''apples with apples,'' surveying buildings of comparable size, age, condition and apartment units.

CHAPTER 3

How To Price Apartment Buildings

"The people who get on in this world are the people who get up and look for the circumstances they want, and, if they can't find them, make them."

—GEORGE BERNARD SHAW

In the preceding chapter, you learned how to survey your local apartment market, obtain firsthand information on rent levels, estimate vacancy rates, judge facilities and amenities and find comparable sales data.

Now we're getting down to numbers that lead to deals.

The next step is determining the *market value* of a specific apartment building. Market value is the price for which an apartment property will sell in the open market if the seller is not under any extreme pressure to sell and the buyer is not under any extreme pressure to buy, with a reasonable period of time allowed the broker to effect the sale.

Four different approaches exist to determining market value, but they all lead to the desired end result: a satisfied buyer and seller, with a nice commission for you.

Before we look at the details, please keep an important fact in mind. All of the price-setting methods apply to every size apartment building. Whether you are dealing with an 8-unit building or one with 200 units, the only difference is the number of zeros in the price.

I use the following methods to arrive at a sound market value:

1. gross rent multiplier
2. capitalization approach
3. price per unit
4. price per square foot

Deciding which method is best in a particular case depends on various factors which will be explained as we move along.

Understanding the basic evaluation methods is extremely important—not only for flexibility in dealing with a wide range of situations, but also to give you that all-important credibility that buyers and sellers will respect.

GROSS RENT MULTIPLIER (GRM) or GROSS INCOME MULTIPLIER (GIM)

This is a popular and highly workable way to evaluate apartment buildings, particularly small- to medium-sized properties.

As the name implies, the GRM is a *number* that multiplies the gross income of an apartment building to arrive at a selling price.

A simple formula shows the relationship between the selling price and the gross scheduled income.

Sales Price = GRM × Gross Income

Gross income is the dollar total of all money produced annually by the apartment property. This figure consists of rental income *plus* any other income sources, such as coin-operated laundry equipment, parking fees, cable or satellite TV service fees and vending machines on the premises.

Example: If a particular apartment building produces $100,000 in annual gross income and the appropriate gross rent multiplier is 8.5, the property would have a market value of 8.5 × $100,000 or $850,000.

Several factors contribute to changes in the numerical value of the gross rent multiplier.

Market Conditions.   The figure (8.5) in the preceding example could drop to a seven or even a five in poor market conditions caused by high vacancy rates, overbuilding of apartments, increased unemployment or other unfavorable trends.

Conversely, the gross rent multiplier could be as high as 10 or 11 if the local real estate market is booming and apartment properties are at a premium because of increased rental demand, inflation or falling interest rates.

As a rule, the GRM will rise in a market with strong population growth, low vacancy rates and favorable financing terms. The GRM, of course, tends to drop in a market with slow appreciation rates, a static population, declining property values and other negative factors.

Certain property characteristics also can cause the gross rent multiplier to vary for specific types of apartment complexes. The following are the most important variables.

Location.   Like all residential properties, apartment building value is strongly influenced by the quality of the neighborhood in which the building is situated. The best locations—luxury apartments fronting the ocean or a lake, for instance—command the highest gross rent multipliers, which are bolstered by better prospects for property appreciation and lower investment risks.

Subjective worth.   A property purchased for owner occupancy can have an above-average multiplier because of personal value to a specific buyer. For example, if a buyer wants to live in the apartment building, he or she may be willing to pay a higher price than a buyer who doesn't plan to live in the building. Other intangibles that can raise the gross rent multiplier may be distinctive architecture or unique amenities.

Age of the building.   Apartment buildings with lower operating expenses usually have a higher gross rent multiplier. Newer buildings require less maintenance than older ones and therefore normally sell at above-average multipliers.

Size of units.   Small dwelling units (apartment units of below average size) have limited tenant appeal and fairly high turnover rates. Buildings with predominantly studio or bachelor units, for instance, tend to attract interim renters who will move out as soon as they can find larger living space. Gross rent multipliers for buildings with a large portion of smaller units are therefore usually lower.

Services provided.   In buildings where the owner provides utilities, furniture and other amenities, operating costs are considerably higher than in buildings where the tenants pay for utilities and supply their own furnishings. The more costly the services provided by the owner, the lower the gross rent multiplier.

Total units.   The number of units in an apartment complex tends to affect the gross rent multiplier because size is related to operating efficiency. Smaller complexes can usually be maintained with lower operating expenses than larger buildings. For example, large properties may have pools, tennis courts and other amenities that are costly to operate and are not usually present in smaller complexes. Also, while the resident manager of a small apartment building can probably maintain the landscaping of the property himself, the grounds of a large complex will most likely require the services of a landscape maintenance company. The result is that large buildings tend to sell at multipliers that are lower than average.

How do you determine the appropriate GRM for a particular property? The answer is easy: the marketplace determines it for you. Now you can put the comparable sales data to work that you have collected, as described in Chapter 2.

Simply review the prices and corresponding gross incomes of at least three *similar* apartment buildings that have sold within the past six months. Figures for apartments that were purchased several years ago are useless in a constantly changing marketplace.

Remember the basic rule of comparing apples with apples. Make sure that the sales you are reviewing apply to apartments that are truly comparable to the property you want to evaluate. They should be similar in size, condition, location and amenities.

Once you know the sales price and gross income of the comparable properties, you can easily determine the GRM applicable to the apartment building you are pricing.

Just convert our earlier formula from multiplication to division. Instead of *Sales Price* = *GRM* × *Gross Income*, use

$$GRM = \frac{Sales\ Price}{Gross\ Income}$$

At this point, you are ready to use your rental survey information described in Chapter 2 because all gross income figures must be reconstructed to reflect *current market rents.*

When you analyze comparable sales data to determine an appropriate GRM, you must use the prevailing market rents at the time of the sale. The reason is that actual rents are often above or below true market-rent levels. Therefore, basing a sales value or GRM on rents that do not reflect existing market conditions at the time of sale can greatly distort the selling price.

Since the best way to learn anything is by actually doing it, let's work out a typical example of using the gross rent multiplier approach to pricing an apartment building. While you do the actual work, I'll coach you from the sidelines. We will make certain assumptions regarding rental rates and GRM values as we go through the price-setting process.

You are going to analyze the 20-unit Colonial Arms apartments for a client who has asked you to determine the most realistic sales price. Your client has provided you with the following information about the building:

Unit Type	Number of This Type	Existing Monthly Rent	Total Income
1 bedroom/1 bath	10	$375	$ 3,750
2 bedroom/1 bath	5	425	2,125
2 bedroom/2 bath	5	450	2,250
		Laundry income monthly	100
		Gross income monthly	8,225
		Gross income annually	$98,700

In your analysis, you must first determine whether the existing rents are at fair market value. Reviewing your rental survey information shows you that units in other buildings of comparable location, quality and size are renting for $400, $440 and $465, respectively. Thus, you know that the units in the building you are pricing are underrented.

Basing your analysis on unrealistic or outdated figures rather than on the potential income that is readily obtainable can greatly distort the value of the property. Therefore, the next step is to reconstruct the gross income by using *market* rents. The resulting new annual total is called the *projected* gross income.

Reconstructed Income Statement Using Market Rents

Unit Type	Number of This Type	Existing Rents	Market Rents	Total Income Monthly Using Market Rents
1 bedroom/1 bath	10	$375	$400	$4,000
2 bedroom/1 bath	5	425	440	2,200
2 bedroom/2 bath	5	450	465	2,325
			Laundry income monthly	100
			Projected gross income monthly	8,625
			Projected gross income annually	$103,500

You're almost home. Next, apply the appropriate gross rent multiplier to the projected annual income. The result will give you the selling price of the property.

Researching recent sales of apartment buildings comparable to the Colonial Arms in location, condition, size and other points of similarity showed you that the other buildings all have sold for about eight times their gross income. (Don't forget to adjust also the gross incomes of the comparable sales to reflect market rents at the time of sale.)

Remember the formula for finding the GRM from comparable sales data.

$$GRM = \frac{Sales\ Price}{Gross\ Income}$$

Multiplying the projected gross annual income of $103,500 by eight gives you a value of $828,000 (Sales Price = GRM × Gross Income).

Before you deem your valuation complete, it may be necessary to make an adjustment in price for buildings that will require large rental increases to reach market rates. Any time apartment owners contemplate a rental increase, they must also anticipate the possibility that some tenants may vacate the building because of the increased rates. The number of tenants who move out will depend on the amount of the rental increase and the availability of competing apartments in the area. Whenever a tenant turnover occurs, the owners can expect to incur certain expenses. These costs include loss of rents during the turnaround period from one tenant to the next, together with refurbishment expenses associated with preparing an apartment for a new tenant. Refurbishment costs are comprised of cleaning, painting, repairs and, if necessary, replacement of carpets, drapes and appliances. Because you've arrived at the building's value using market rents, you will need to subtract from that value an allowance for any substantial tenant turnover costs associated with obtaining those rents.

In cases of a modest rent increase, such as the $15 to $25 per unit in the preceding example, you would most likely expect only a small tenant turnover and probably would not need to make an allowance in the price of the building.

However, if you were working with a building that was $50 to $100 per unit underrented, you might expect a large turnover since many of the tenants might not be able to afford the new market rents.

Let's assume that the Colonial Arms is substantially underrented and consequently you have predicted that half of the apartments will undergo a tenant turnover. What costs will be incurred in bringing the rents to market levels? First, your market knowledge tells you that in the area in which this building is located it takes approximately two weeks to rerent an apartment once a tenant vacates. Assuming an average rental rate of $400 per month per unit, the total loss of rents will come to $2,000. (Ten apartments vacant for two weeks each equals 20 vacant weeks. At an average of $100 per week the total loss of rents is $2,000.)

Second, you've also discovered that five of the soon-to-be-vacated apartments will need new carpets, drapes and paint at an expenditure of $1,500 per unit. The total refurbishment costs for these five units equals $7,500. The other five units will need little, if any, work. In this example, total costs associated with bringing rental rates to market levels come to $9,500. Subtracting $9,500 from the indicated sales price of $828,000 gives you a final market value of $818,500.

From this scenario, it's obviously a good idea to ask to see some of the apartment interiors any time building owners request that you determine the market value of their property. If it is not possible to gain access to the units, you should, at the very least, ask the owners about the condition of the apartment interiors. In this way, you can determine if an allowance in price will need to be made for any refurbishment costs. (We'll discuss inspecting apartment interiors in more detail in Chapter 12.)

Before we move on, let's quickly summarize the steps necessary to find the market value of an apartment building using the gross rent multiplier approach.

1. Memorize the equation for determining market value using the gross rent multiplier method:

$$Sales\ Price\ =\ GRM\ \times\ Gross\ Income$$

2. Reconstruct the gross income of the building being evaluated using current market rents.
3. Analyze the pertinent data from recent sales of comparable apartment buildings to select the appropriate GRM. Remember that the numerical value of the GRM is influenced by certain market conditions and property characteristics. Adjust the gross incomes of the comparable buildings to reflect market rents at the time of sale.
4. If necessary, make an allowance in the sales price for any substantial costs associated with bringing the rents to market rates.

For additional practice using the gross rent multiplier and the other pricing methods you're about to learn, work out the pricing problems at the end of this chapter.

CAPITALIZATION APPROACH

Investors also frequently use the capitalization approach to determine the market value of an apartment building. Institutional buyers and sellers, such as life insurance companies and pension fund managers, particularly favor this method of pricing larger apartment properties.

The capitalization method lets you determine the market value of an apartment building by dividing the building's *net income* (also referred to as *net operating income*) by an appropriate rate of return on the buyer's investment. The rate of return is called the capitalization (cap) rate and is expressed as a *percentage*. Here is the simple equation:

$$Sales\ Price\ =\ \frac{Net\ Income}{Cap\ Rate}$$

Example: If a 30-unit apartment building produces $90,000 in net annual income and the appropriate cap rate is nine percent, the property would have a market value of $90,000 divided by .09, or $1 million.

The same market variables that cause numerical changes in the gross rent multiplier also can change the cap rate. However, unlike GRMs, the rise or fall in the cap rate is *inversely* related to fluctuations in the marketplace. As market conditions strengthen, cap rates decline; as market trends weaken, cap rates rise. This relationship means that investors will demand a higher rate of return in a poor market where risks are greater.

Remember, when using the capitalization approach, we will be working with a building's *net income* instead of with its gross income (as was the case with the gross rent multiplier method).

You can easily calculate the net income of an apartment building by following four steps.

Step 1. As in the GRM method, determine the projected gross annual income using market rents.

Step 2. Subtract from the gross income an allowance for vacancies. For instance, if the area in which the building is located is experiencing an eight-percent vacancy rate, subtract eight percent from the gross income.

How do you find the vacancy rate in your area? By doing your rental survey. (Refer to Chapter 2.)

By subtracting the vacancy allowance from the gross income, you have arrived at the *effective* gross income.

Example:

Total gross income	$100,000
less eight percent vacancy rate	– 8,000
Effective gross income	$ 92,000

Step 3. The next step is to determine the annual expenses of the building. These costs are separated into two categories: fixed expenses and operating expenses.

Fixed expenses—such as insurance premiums and property taxes—are those costs that remain fairly constant over a period of time.

Insurance coverage for apartment buildings normally consists of fire and public liability. Special provisions may also cover the loss of rents due to fire, flood or other events that render the apartment units uninhabitable. Insurance premiums depend on the type of coverage, the kinds of construction materials used in the building and the location of the property. Premiums also can vary greatly from one insurance company to another. A good idea is to consult with a number of insurance agents in your area to find out which companies are the most competitive in providing apartment building policies.

The formula for determining property taxes—another fixed expense—can vary from state to state, with special bond assessments in one county differing from those in another county. If you're not already familiar with the assessment procedures in your area, contact the local tax assessor's office for full information.

Operating expenses are the ongoing costs of running the apartment building. Besides management fees or salaries, these expenses include utilities, pool cleaning, landscape maintenance, trash collection service, pest control and building repairs.

The cost of management can differ greatly from building to building and is determined by the type and size of the property and by the needs of the owner. Supervision of smaller apartment properties usually is conducted by a resident manager. His or her compensation will vary according to the number of apartment units in the complex and he or she is often paid in the form of free rent. The manager's duties normally include showing and renting the apartments, collecting the rents, performing minor maintenance and repair work and keeping the premises clean.

At times, particularly in the case of larger complexes, an owner may employ the services of a professional property management company to supervise the resident manager, keep financial records and perform other administrative functions for the building. Property management fees can range from four percent to eight percent of the collected monthly rents.

Utility expenses include gas, electricity, water and sewer service. If the apartments have separate utility meters, the tenants will pay for the use of gas and electricity inside their units with the owner providing power for the common areas (outdoor lighting, laundry room utilities, swimming pool heaters and so on).

Building repairs consist of cleaning and painting the apartment interiors and providing proper maintenance to all building systems including plumbing and electrical.

Important: When calculating expenses you must determine the costs that the *new* owner will incur. These expenses can be very different from those the previous owner may have experienced.

For instance, property taxes ordinarily are set by an *ad valorem* (according to value) schedule. The new owner may face higher property taxes to reflect the price he or she has paid for the building. The buyer may also incur larger premiums for more comprehensive liability insurance or may feel a need to increase repair expenses for a building that has not been properly maintained.

To gain quickly and easily the expertise you'll need in projecting apartment expenses, I suggest you obtain an excellent publication from the Institute of Real Estate Management of the National Association of Realtors. The book is updated annually and is called *Income/Expense Analysis: Apartments*. This valuable reference contains a detailed analysis of the operating experience of over 5,500 multifamily properties across the United States and Canada. The data are summarized by building type for over 100 major metropolitan markets, and cover all the primary sources of revenue and categories of expenses in operating apartment buildings. The information is given to you in the form of income and expenses per square foot of building area. This format allows you to make an easy comparison between the performance of the properties surveyed and the one you want to analyze.

You can order a copy of *Income/Expense Analysis: Apartments* by writing or phoning the Institute of Real Estate Management, 430 North Michigan Avenue, Chicago, IL 60611-4090; telephone 312-661-1930.

Step 4. To complete the capitalization approach to pricing apartment buildings, subtract the total of the projected expenses from the effective gross income to arrive at the net operating income.

Here is an example of the full calculation using a 40-unit apartment building with a projected gross annual income of $200,000.

Projected gross annual income		$200,000
less vacancy allowance (8%)		− 16,000
Effective gross income		$184,000
Projected expenses:		
Management	$ 9,500	
Taxes	15,000	
Insurance	2,500	
Water	7,300	
Gas and electricity	9,600	
Maintenance and repairs	10,000	
Pool service	1,200	
Pest control service	600	
Trash removal	1,400	
Gardener	3,600	
Supplies	3,700	
Less total expenses		− 64,400
Net operating income		$119,600

With a little practice in your marketplace, you'll soon be able to estimate projected expenses as a percentage of the effective gross income for any apartment building. This ability will greatly help you when you quickly want to reach a "ballpark" value using the capitalization approach. In our example, the expenses are 35 percent of the effective gross income.

Now you are ready to determine market value by applying the appropriate cap rate to the net operating income. What is the appropriate cap rate? Once again, it's back to basics.

As in the GRM method, you simply look at comparable sales data. *Reminder*: When you are analyzing comparable sales to find cap rates, correct the gross income to reflect *market rents* at the time of sale and estimate the expenses that the *new owner* would have anticipated.

By subtracting the expenses from the gross income, you will arrive at the net income. You can determine the cap rates of recently sold comparable properties by manipulating the previous equation and dividing the net income by the sales price.

$$Cap\ Rate = \frac{Net\ Income}{Sales\ Price}$$

Assuming that comparable buildings are selling at eight-percent cap rates, the building would have a market value of

$119,600 ÷ .08, or $1,495,000.

As with the gross rent multiplier method, you should subtract an allowance from this figure for any tenant turnover and necessary refurbishment costs required to bring rental rates to market levels.

Here's a quick review of the capitalization approach:

1. Remember the equation for determining market value using the capitalization method:

$$Sales\ Price = \frac{Net\ Income}{Cap\ Rate}$$

2. Determine net income by subtracting a vacancy allowance and expenses from the gross income. Remember to reconstruct rents to reflect market rates and project expenses to reflect the costs that the new owner will incur.

3. Analyze recent comparable sales and determine the appropriate cap rate to apply to the net income. Make sure you've adjusted rents to market levels at the time of sale and projected expenses the new owner would have to anticipate.

4. Make an allowance in the property price for any substantial costs associated with bringing below-market rents to prevailing rent levels.

Understanding the gross rent multiplier and capitalization methods of setting apartment prices gives you an important advantage in dealing with sellers and buyers. Both of these approaches are easy to learn; therefore, you'll soon be using them with virtually no effort at all.

PRICE PER UNIT

This is a technique that is a real time saver when you need to make a quick estimate of apartment market values. It is the least sophisticated of all the price-setting methods, but it is one you'll use again and again as a starting point for a more thorough evaluation later.

The price per unit method is this easy: Divide the price of the apartment building by the number of units it contains.

$$Price\ Per\ Unit = \frac{Sales\ Price}{Number\ of\ Units}$$

Example: A ten-unit building sells for $380,000. Price per unit is $380,000 divided by ten units, or $38,000 per unit. To obtain the selling price of the property, just multiply the number of units by the appropriate price per unit:

$$Sales\ Price = Number\ of\ Units \times Price\ Per\ Unit$$

What is the "appropriate" price per unit? Now we're back to *comparables* again. What are similar units in similar locations selling for?

Important: When using the price per unit method as with the other price-setting techniques, be sure you are comparing like properties. As you learned when making your rental survey (Chapter 2), apartment buildings can vary considerably in their unit mixes. A building comprised of all one-bedroom apartments is not going to sell at the same price per unit as a building consisting of two- and three-bedroom units.

By doing your basic market research homework and using this method, you'll soon be an "instant expert" on approximating apartment building values.

I emphasize that the price per unit method is not a precise technique and should be used only for a quick estimate of value. A serious analysis should always be backed up by the gross rent multiplier or capitalization method.

PRICE PER SQUARE FOOT

This is another helpful technique you can use to reach a quick estimate of value. It is similar to the price per unit method but not quite so easy to use because you need to know the amount of *rentable* square footage for the entire building. The rentable square footage is the total square footage of the interior space of all the apartment units. It does not include interior hallways, elevator shafts or other common areas that do not collect income. Unfortunately, the amount of rentable square footage in a building is a figure that is not always readily available. However, if you are able to ascertain the square footages of the various unit types, you can calculate the total rentable area in the building. Be sure you know this method because some sellers—like builders who construct apartment buildings for sale upon completion—tend to think in terms of cost per square foot.

Example: With the following information, you could easily find the total rentable square footage in this 25-unit building.

No. of Units	Unit Type	Square Footage of Unit Type	Total Square Footage
10	1 bedroom/1 bath	650	6,500
10	2 bedroom/2 bath	850	8,500
5	3 bedroom/2 bath	1,000	5,000
	Total rentable square footage		20,000 sq. ft.

The equation for determining price per square foot is:

$$Price\ Per\ Square\ Foot = \frac{Sales\ Price}{Total\ Rentable\ Square\ Feet}$$

In the above example, if the building had a market value of $1 million, the price per square foot would be $1 million divided by 20,000 square feet, or $50 per square foot.

Once again, your comparable sales data will tell you what comparable buildings in similar areas are selling for in terms of price per square foot. (*Note:* When using the price per square foot method, be particularly careful to compare properties of similar construction materials. The cost per foot of a steel frame highrise will differ greatly from that of a two-story wood frame building. This may seem like an elementary point, but often it's the obvious that we overlook.

Learn the four methods of pricing apartments. You'll use all of them at one time or another. They are tested proven ways to help put buyers and sellers together without guesswork.

And where will all this leave you? Exactly where you want to be—right in the middle of a big fat commission! To get into the swing of things, let's do the following exercises.

APARTMENT PRICING EXERCISES

Problem 1

The Villa Royal is a ten-unit apartment building with five 2-bedroom/2-bath units renting for $500 per month and five 1 bedroom/1 bath apartments renting for $395 per month. Laundry income is $50 per month. The rents are all $15 below market rates and comparable properties in the area are selling at 8.3 times gross income. Determine the value of the Villa Royal using the gross rent multiplier method.

Problem 2

The 15-unit Cypress Manor Apartments contains eight 1-bedroom/1-bath units renting for $400 per month, five 2-bedroom/1-bath units renting for $475 per month, and two 3-bedroom/2-bath units renting for $550 per month. Laundry income is $75 per month. The rental rates are at market levels, the vacancy rate in the area is 5 percent and the new owner is anticipating expenses at 33 percent of the effective gross income. If comparable apartment buildings in the area are selling at 9 percent cap rates, calculate the value of the Cypress Manor using the capitalization method.

Problem 3

An eight-unit apartment building recently sold for $350,000. The gross income at the time of sale was $43,000 based on market rental rates. Vacancy in the area is 4 percent and the new owner can expect expenses of 32 percent of effective gross income. Derive the gross rent multiplier and cap rate of this sale for your comparable sales data file.

SOLUTIONS

Problem 1

Step 1.   Since the apartment units are underrented, you must determine the gross income of the building using market rents.

Unit Type	Number of This Type	Existing Rents	Market Rents	Total Income Monthly Using Market Rents
1 bedroom/1 bath	5	$395	$410	$ 2,050
2 bedroom/2 bath	5	500	515	2,575
		Laundry income monthly		50
		Projected gross income monthly		4,675
		Projected gross income annually		$56,100

Step 2. Applying the gross rent multiplier of 8.3 to the projected gross income gives you a valuation of $465,630.

Problem 2

Step 1. Since rents are already at market levels, begin by calculating the existing gross income.

Unit Type	Number of This Type	Existing Rents	Total Income
1 bedroom/1 bath	8	$400	$ 3,200
2 bedroom/1 bath	5	475	2,375
3 bedroom/2 bath	2	550	75
		Laundry income monthly	75
		Gross income monthly	6,750
		Gross income annually	$81,000

Step 2. Subtract the appropriate allowance for vacancy and expenses.

Gross income annually	$81,000
less vacancy (5%)	– 4,050
Effective gross income	$76,950
less expenses (33%)	– 25,393
Net operating income	$51,557

Step 3. Divide the net operating income by the appropriate cap rate, as determined by your comparable sales data, to arrive at the indicated value. (In this example we are using a nine-percent cap rate).

$$\frac{\$51,557}{.09} = \$572,855$$

Problem 3

Step 1.   To determine the gross rent multiplier of a given sale property, divide the sales price by the gross income. Given a $350,000 sales price and a gross income of $43,000, the gross rent multiplier is 8.14.

$$\frac{\$350,000}{\$43,000} = 8.14$$

Step 2.   To find the cap rate at the time of sale, begin by subtracting the vacancy allowance from the gross income to determine the effective gross income. Subtract expenses from the effective gross income to arrive at the net operating income. Then, divide the sales price by the net operating income.

Gross income	$43,000
less vacancy (4%)	− 1,720
Effective income	$41,280
less expenses (33%)	− 13,622
Net operating income	$27,658

$$\frac{\$27,658}{\$350,000} = 7.9\% \text{ cap rate}$$

(In this problem, rents were already at market levels. However, when rents are not at market rates, you must adjust the gross income to reflect market rents at the time of sale.)

SUMMING UP WHAT YOU'VE LEARNED IN CHAPTER 3

Knowing the market value of an apartment property results in a price at which the building is most likely to sell in prevailing market conditions. Review the following points is this chapter.

1. The four methods of arriving at a sound market value are the gross rent multiplier, the capitalization approach, price per unit and price per square foot.

2. When determining the market value of an apartment building, use *market* rents, not actual rents, which may be above or below prevailing levels.

3. An adjustment in price may be necessary for needed replacements of carpeting, appliances, water heaters and other costly items.

4. The annual costs of an apartment building consist of fixed expenses, such as taxes and insurance, and operating expenses, such as utilities, pool cleaning, trash collection service and building repairs.

5. When calculating expenses, determine the costs that the *new* owner will incur. These can vary greatly from the costs that the previous owner may have paid.

6. If you use the price per unit or price per square foot methods to get a quick ballpark estimate, be sure to use the GRM or Capitalization methods for more accuracy in your final evaluation.

4

Financing

"Business? It's quite simple. It's other people's money."

—ALEXANDRE DUMAS
THE YOUNGER

By this time, you've come pretty far in learning about selling apartments. You now know how to survey the rental market, how to gain comparable sales data, how to price apartments and other essentials to get you started.

Now we're going to look at ways of financing apartment buildings. In Chapter 2 we noted the importance of understanding financing. In this chapter we will describe how and why various lending arrangements are used.

If you have never dealt with real estate financing, what follows will serve as a basic introduction to the subject. If you are an experienced real estate broker or agent, please view this chapter as a miniature refresher course. Speaking for myself, I find that no matter how much I have learned about a subject, reviewing the basics from time to time reinforces the importance of fundamentals. The better you understand and use primary guidelines, the better you can stay on a profitable course for your future.

BREAK EVEN OR CASH FLOW

In the preceding chapter we computed the gross income and subtracted from it an allowance for vacancies and an amount for expenses. This computation gave us the net operating income (NOI). Let's now extend the operating statement one step further to include the financing payments. The net operating income is the amount of income that is left to make the loan payments (debt service). If the net operating income equals the debt service the building will be "breaking even." If income remains after the loan payments have been made, the building is producing a "pretax cash flow." The pretax cash flow is the amount of income available to the investor before the payment of income taxes. (We'll deal with income taxes and the after-tax cash flow in the next chapter.)

Obviously, if there is not enough NOI to cover the debt service, the buyer will have a *negative cash flow*. This means, of course, that the buyer will have to pay some of the monthly loan amount from cash sources other than the apartment building.

Example: Given a 20-unit apartment building with a gross annual income of $110,000, 5 percent vacancy, 35 percent operating expense and a 30-year loan of $560,000 at 10 percent interest, our operating statement would now look like this:

Gross income	$110,000
less vacancy (5%)	−5,500
Effective gross income	104,500
less operating expenses (35%)	−36,575
Net operating income	67,925
less debt service (12 months)	−59,002
Cash flow (before taxes)	$ 8,923

Dividing the cash flow by the amount of the down payment gives you the "spendable" or the "cash on cash" return to the investor. Assuming an $800,000 purchase price and a $240,000 down payment, the spendable return in this example would be 3.72 percent ($8,923/$240,000 = 3.72%).

Determining the loan payments for a given loan amount is a simple process. You need only refer to a loan amortization table (one is provided at the end of this chapter) to find the appropriate *mortgage constant*. The mortgage constant is the factor that is multiplied by the amount of the loan to determine the loan payments required to amortize the loan over the term of repayment as well as to pay the interest on the unpaid balance. Look across the top of the amortization schedule to locate the interest rate being charged on the loan. Go down the interest rate column until you find the mortgage constant that corresponds to the appropriate loan term. In the preceding example, the monthly loan constant for a 10 percent, 30-year loan is .00878.

Thus:

*.00878 × $560,000 = $4,916.80 monthly payment × 12 = $59,002
(rounded) annual debt service.*

You can calculate the monthly debt service much faster using a handheld financial calculator that contains a built-in amortization program.

You can also use the amortization table and mortgage constant to determine the maximum amount of debt that an apartment building can support and still break even. To do so, divide the net operating income by 12 to obtain the monthly income available for loan payments. Then divide the monthly income figure by the appropriate mortgage constant to arrive at the loan amount. Thus, an apartment building with an annual NOI of $70,000 could support a 9.5 percent, 30-year loan in the maximum amount of $693,600 and still break even (annual NOI of $70,000/12 = $5,833 monthly NOI; $5,833/.00841 mortgage constant for 9.5 percent interest, 30-yr. term = $693,600 loan amount).

The percentage of net operating income needed to service the debt on a particular building is called the ''debt coverage ratio'' (DCR) and is found by dividing the net operating income by the debt service. In the preceding scenario, where the net operating income is equal to the debt service, the debt coverage ratio is one. Lending institutions use the debt coverage ratio as a measurement of risk because it determines the property's ability to make the loan payments. Lenders will require increased debt coverage ratios when adverse market conditions, such as higher vacancy rates or declining property values, are anticipated for apartment properties. A higher debt coverage ratio results in a lower loan amount.

Determining the amount of financing that a lender will make against a given apartment building is a three-step process. First, divide the net operating income by 12 to obtain the monthly NOI. Second, divide the monthly NOI by the required debt coverage ratio. (As part of your market knowledge, you should stay up-to-date on lenders' debt coverage requirements). Third, divide the resulting income allowed by the lender for debt service by the appropriate monthly mortgage constant.

Example: If an apartment building is producing a net operating income of $35,000 and prevailing loan rates are 10-percent interest, 30-year amortization, with a 1.1 debt coverage ratio, the lender would finance $302,000.

$$\frac{\$35,000\ NOI}{12} = \$2,917\ monthly\ NOI$$

$$\frac{\$2,917}{1.1\ (DCR)} = \$2,652\ income\ allowable\ for\ debt\ service$$

$$\frac{\$2,652}{.00878\ constant} = \$302,000\ loan\ amount.$$

Assuming a $400,000 purchase price and no additional seller financing, a buyer would have to put down $98,000 ($400,000 – $302,000) to complete the transaction. This down payment represents 24.5 percent of the total sale amount ($98,000/ $400,000).

LEVERAGE

Investors will finance an apartment building according to their investment objectives. Many investors favor borrowing as much as possible so that investing in income-producing property requires minimum equity capital. They are using the principle of "financial leverage" to maximize the rate of return on their invested dollars. Defined simply, leverage is the technique of purchasing real estate with borrowed money—as when buying stocks on margin.

Remember your high school physics course? The longer the lever, the greater the weight that can be lifted. In buying real estate, the greater the amount of borrowed funds relative to the buyer's invested capital, the greater the leverage. Investors are willing to assume a large debt because they believe the rate of return earned by the building will be greater than the cost of the borrowed money.

Let's see how this principle works. An investor purchases an apartment building for $600,000. The building is producing a $55,000 net operating income. We'll assume that he sells the building after one year and makes a $30,000 profit.

Example 1 (no leverage): If the investor had purchased the property entirely with his own money and used no financing, he would receive a 14.16 percent pretax rate of return on his invested funds.

NOI	$55,000
– debt service	0
Cash flow	55,000
+ appreciation	30,000
Profit	$85,000

$85,000 divided by $600,000 equals a pretax rate of return of 14.16 percent.

Example 2 (leverage): If the buyer invested $150,000 and borrowed $450,000 at 10-percent interest and a 30-year term, his pretax rate of return would *increase to 25.07 percent.*

NOI	$55,000	
– debt service	47,389	($450,000 @ 10%,
Cash flow	7,611	30 yrs.)
+ appreciation	30,000	
Profit	$37,611	

$37,611 divided by $150,000 equals a pretax rate of return of 25.07 percent.

Thus, you can see how the use of leverage can be a powerful tool to help investors increase the return on their invested dollars. This is particularly true in times of high inflation. Not only does the investor gain by the sharp rise in property values, he or she benefits at the lender's expense by repaying the debt with cheaper dollars.

However, the use of leverage is not without its drawbacks. A major disadvantage is that the gain produced by leverage is accompanied by a corresponding rise in the level of financial risk for the investor. Because increased borrowing means a larger debt service, there may be a higher probability of default on the loan.

Since few investors purchase properties entirely with their own funds (insurance companies and pension funds are the major exceptions), you will find leverage used to a degree in almost all apartment transactions.

What is the appropriate amount of leverage for an investor to use? The answer depends on the buyer's investment objectives, his or her tolerance for risk and prevailing real estate market conditions.

Investors desiring to receive income from their properties use less leverage in order to lower debt service and increase cash flow. Others, hoping to realize large gains from appreciation at the time of sale, are willing to forego cash flow benefits and use more leverage to increase the rate of return on their invested dollars.

However, in times of high interest rates, the concept of leverage is much more difficult to apply. As interest rates rise, the net operating income of a building will service a smaller amount of debt. Therefore, unless property prices come down or the seller is willing to carry back some of the financing at below-market rates, the investor is forced to use more equity dollars to purchase the property.

High demand for apartment properties can also reduce the amount of leverage available to investors. Competition among buyers during favorable market conditions often reduces the pressure on sellers to carry back secondary financing in addition to primary loan amounts obtainable through conventional sources. An exception, of course, is the owner who is motivated to carry back financing for income tax purposes (we'll discuss tax aspects in the next chapter) or one who wants to acquire interest income from real estate notes.

YOUR PRICE, MY TERMS

Like most large transactions, the sale of an apartment property usually involves a certain amount of give and take on the part of buyer and seller. A serious buyer will often agree to the asking price provided that the seller makes some concessions on the purchase terms, for example, carrying back part of the financing, extending the term of the loan or giving other benefits to the buyer. Hence, the real estate adage, "I'll pay your price, but on my terms."

The terms of a sale (leverage and financing) often can be as important to investors as price in their decision to purchase a particular apartment building. In fact, they can have their own value—a value separate from the one you place on the property using the appraisal techniques we discussed in the last chapter.

The availability of below-market-rate financing or increased leverage may motivate buyers to pay a higher price for a specific property if the favorable terms allow them to achieve their desired investment objectives. On the other hand, unfavorable terms can cause a discount in value or preclude a sale altogether. Therefore, when you are analyzing a prospective apartment building for acquisition or sale, you also need to consider any proposed terms to determine whether they add or subtract from the building's value. While analyzing financing terms is not a method for pricing an apartment building, understanding the terms of a sale can help you make any needed adjustments in the property's market value, which may be affected by certain financing conditions.

Study the sale terms of the comparable sales data that you collect. That way, you can determine the prevailing amount of leverage and the types of financing that are being used in your marketplace. You should also see what effect these terms are having on the operating statements and sales prices of the comparable properties. Are the prevailing terms producing a break-even situation, a positive cash flow, or even possibly a negative cash flow? Will a 25 percent down payment produce a break-even status? If so, how does that compare with other apartment transactions taking place in your market? This analysis is important because it provides a benchmark to help you and your clients determine the value of the proposed terms of a particular transaction. You may learn of a property selling at a seemingly high price, only to find out that the investor bought the property with a very low down payment and the seller carried back the financing at below-market interest rates. You could also be working on a building that will only break even with a 30-percent down payment, while comparable properties are showing a five percent spendable return with that percentage cash down. In those circumstances you might conclude that the building is priced too high or the financing is too expensive.

Remember, too, that conditions vary from marketplace to marketplace. While apartment buildings in one area may be selling with certain prevailing terms and spendable returns, the scenario could be completely different in another area. Know *your* market!

Now let's take a look at some of the various types of financing available to apartment investors.

CONVENTIONAL LOANS

The largest share of apartment lending is done through so-called conventional sources. Conventional financing means loans made by institutional lenders without government guarantees. "Institutionals" pool their depositors' money and then invest it in mortgages and trust deeds. These lenders consist of savings and loan associations, commercial banks, insurance companies and mutual savings banks.

Savings and loan associations fund the majority of long-term apartment mortgages. Commercial banks tend to favor short-term loans and normally provide only construction financing for new apartment buildings. Insurance companies are also apartment lenders, but normally only make major loans of $2 million and up, and preferably above $5 million.

ALTERNATIVE FINANCING

Until recently, most real estate transactions were financed with a fixed-interest-rate loan. This method was particularly beneficial to apartment investors. If their apartment building was successful in the years following its purchase and the net operating income increased over that period of time, the pretax cash flow would also increase because the debt service payment and interest rate remained constant. However, the high inflation and interest rate levels of the late 1970s and early 1980s have changed the attitude of institutional lenders who are now wary of fixed-rate loans. Since then, financing instruments such as variable-rate mortgages and participation mortgages have gained in popularity with the financial institutions because these methods provide the lender a degree of protection from inflation and rapidly fluctuating interest rates.

Although most investors would prefer a fixed-rate loan, alternative financing methods can provide an opportunity for the investor to borrow at lower interest rates (at least initially) than might be available with a fixed-rate loan. Since investor and lender share the risks of unexpected inflation and rising interest rates, these negative elements need not be taken into account to the same extent in variable-rate instruments as in fixed-rate loans.

A profile follows of some of the alternative financing methods with which you should become familiar. You're not expected to be the "Loan Arranger" for apartment buyers, but you'll ride taller in the saddle when you're confident about your financial knowledge.

VARIABLE-RATE MORTGAGES

These lending instruments, also known as adjustable-rate mortgages and renegotiable-rate loans, are financing plans in which the interest rate can increase or decrease over time, according to a standard index. Changes in the interest rate may also reflect a change in the payment, the maturity date, the principal loan balance or a combination of all three.

Two common indexes for setting interest levels on variable-rate mortgages (VRMs) are the "cost of money" to lenders from the Federal Home Loan Bank (FHLB) and U.S. government treasury bill auction rates.

Using either of the above guidelines, the lender charges the borrower an interest rate that "floats" a few percentage points above that of the index. The difference between the two interest rates is called the spread. Normally "caps" are written into the loan to establish the maximum and minimum that the interest rate may rise or fall. However, great variation can exist in the extent to which VRM loans protect borrowers against increases in interest costs. Since investors often rely on their brokers to advise them of their financing alternatives, you should keep yourself constantly updated on the entire real estate financing picture.

PARTICIPATION LOANS

Another alternative financing method that you may encounter—especially if you are dealing with developers of new apartment buildings—is the participation loan, or shared appreciation mortgage. Under this loan plan, the lender has a right to participate in an agreed percentage of the income and/or future appreciation in the value of the property used to secure the loan. In exchange for such financial gain, the lender will make the loan at below-market interest or give other favorable concessions to the borrower. These loans can have either fixed or variable interest rates with level or graduated payments.

At this point, you need to be aware of certain factors that are often integral elements of lending agreements.

Collateral Provisions

Real estate loans can contain special clauses or conditions called "collateral provisions" to which the borrower and lender agree when the loan is made. Some of the more common provisions you are likely to meet follow.

Prepayment Penalty. This provision allows the lender to assess a penalty on the borrower if the loan is paid off before its due date. Generally, the prepayment penalty charged will be 6 to 12 months of interest on the balance of the loan. Most lenders will waive this penalty if a subsequent buyer of the property also obtain financing from them. For this reason, sellers with large prepayment penalty provisions in their loans will usually require buyers to seek financing from the same lender as a condition of sale.

Acceleration Clause. This clause gives the lender the right to demand immediate payment of all sums owed to him or her upon the occurrence of certain events. These events can include the borrower's failure to meet monthly payments, nonpayment of property taxes, a failure to maintain the property or other serious negligence.

Alienation Clause. This is a specific type of acceleration clause that makes the loan immediately due and payable if the borrower sells the property before the end of the loan term. This provision is also known as a "due-on-sale" clause.

Lock-in Provision. A lock-in provision specifies a time period from the inception of the loan during which the lender will not allow that the loan be paid off. Generally, lock-in periods have not been used in loans made by banks and savings and loan associations, but sometimes have been imposed by life insurance companies, pension funds and some savings banks.

Real estate loans can also contain provisions in addition to the ones we've just reviewed. Your clients should read all their loan documents carefully to be sure they understand completely all the clauses involved. (*Note:* It's a good idea for you, as a salesperson, to review the existing loan documents on a property that you are attempting to sell to make sure there are no clauses that could adversely affect your sales transaction later on.)

SELLER FINANCING

Quite often, sellers of real estate will "carry back" part of the purchase price themselves. In essence, the seller is becoming a lender to the buyer. In most cases, owner carry-back financing is done to help fund the purchase and to expedite the sale, but in some cases it can also be done for income tax purposes. (We'll cover this when we explain installment sales in the next chapter.)

Usually, seller financing takes the form of a second trust deed or mortgage (although thirds and sometimes fourths are not uncommon). This supplementary financing is generally for a shorter period of time—normally three to seven years—than a first trust deed or mortgage. However, the maturity period can be for any length of time agreed on by both buyer and seller.

When it is beneficial to preserve existing below-market-rate financing, a seller may take back a *wraparound* or *all-inclusive* mortgage, which includes, but is subordinated to, the existing financing. With this arrangement, the seller continues to service the debt on the existing loans by using the payments made on the "wrap" by the buyer. This type of mortgage should not be used, however, if any existing liens contain due-on-sale provisions. Because of the complexities involved, both buyer and seller should consult competent legal counsel any time the use of a wraparound mortgage is considered.

YOUR BEST GUIDE: *YOU*

At the outset of this chapter, I said our discussion of financing would be basic and brief. And so it is. No book, seminar or course of study could cover all the variables that affect the funding of apartment sales. It is especially impossible for any one reference source to describe real estate circumstances in all areas.

Marketplaces, like people, have individual and often peculiar characteristics. And only *you* can learn the pertinent facts about your particular market. Therefore, I repeat my earlier suggestion that you collect your own information about the real estate territory in which you're going to build your apartment sales career.

With the market knowledge you've already gained, you're ready to start establishing yourself as a walking information center in your sphere of business. And what an advantage that is! You'll be in control of your sales activity, and as time goes on you can become recognized as an authoritative source of apartment sale transactions. You'll also find yourself doing creative "what if" thinking. What if the seller would carry back part of the financing? What if your buyer who can't swing a deal by himself would team up with another investor? What if your client obtained secondary financing from an institutional lender?

Your opportunities will be as wide as your imagination and your income will be unlimited. All because you will *know your market*.

Talk to other agents and brokers, visit bankers, introduce yourself to private lenders and study the real estate and financial sections of your local newspaper. Ask questions. Listen. Learn.

The key to your success is market information and how you use it to create sales. That's the fun part of selling apartments. Think of the personal satisfaction and financial rewards you'll enjoy by pairing buyers and sellers in big important transactions. Nothing can replace the exhilaration of being able to say, "I did it!" Gathering local financing information will help you do it. And in your market, you'll be your own best guide.

"But," you say, "isn't financing only part of the money picture for apartment investors? What about tax benefits?"

I'm glad you asked because the next chapter deals with that subject. But don't tense up and grit your teeth. You'll be surprised to learn that sometimes the tax code isn't all that bad.

SUMMING UP WHAT YOU'VE LEARNED
IN CHAPTER 4

Thoroughly understanding how apartment financing works adds greatly to your professionalism in the eyes of your clients. The following are some of the most important facts to know.

1. An apartment building breaks even if the net operating income (NOI) equals the debt service (loan payments).

2. If income remains after the loan payments are made, the building produces a "pretax cash flow."

3. When income is less than the debt service, the buyer will have a negative cash flow.

4. Financial leverage is the technique of buying real estate with borrowed money. The larger the loan in relation to the purchase price, the greater the leverage.

5. Know the prevailing terms used for the financing of apartment buildings in your area. Know what percentage of the purchase price is required for the down payment and how the amount of down payment affects the net operating income.

6. Study the financing documents of existing loans on apartment properties with which you will be working to determine whether there are any collateral provisions that might hinder the sale.

Mortgage Constant Table (Monthly Payments)

Years	7.00%	7.25%	7.50%	7.75%	8.00%	8.25%	Years
			Interest Rate				
1	.08653	.08664	.08676	.08687	.08699	.08710	1
2	.04477	.04489	.04500	.04511	.04523	.04534	2
3	.03088	.03099	.03111	.03122	.03134	.03145	3
4	.02395	.02406	.02418	.02430	.02441	.02453	4
5	.01980	.01992	.02004	.02016	.02028	.02040	5
6	.01705	.01717	.01729	.01741	.01753	.01766	6
7	.01509	.01522	.01534	.01546	.01560	.01571	7
8	.01363	.01376	.01388	.01401	.01414	.01426	8
9	.01251	.01263	.01276	.01289	.01302	.01315	9
10	.01161	.01174	.01187	.01200	.01213	.01227	10
11	.01088	.01102	.01115	.01128	.01142	.01155	11
12	.01028	.01042	.01055	.01069	.01082	.01096	12
13	.00978	.00992	.01005	.01019	.01033	.01047	13
14	.00935	.00949	.00963	.00977	.00991	.01006	14
15	.00899	.00913	.00927	.00941	.00956	.00970	15
16	.00867	.00881	.00896	.00910	.00925	.00940	16
17	.00840	.00854	.00869	.00883	.00898	.00913	17
18	.00816	.00830	.00845	.00860	.00875	.00890	18
19	.00794	.00809	.00824	.00839	.00855	.00870	19
20	.00775	.00790	.00806	.00821	.00836	.00862	20
21	.00758	.00774	.00789	.00805	.00820	.00836	21
22	.00743	.00759	.00775	.00790	.00806	.00822	22
23	.00730	.00746	.00761	.00777	.00793	.00810	23
24	.00718	.00734	.00750	.00766	.00782	.00798	24
25	.00707	.00723	.00739	.00755	.00772	.00788	25
26	.00697	.00713	.00729	.00746	.00763	.00779	26
27	.00688	.00704	.00721	.00737	.00754	.00771	27
28	.00680	.00696	.00713	.00730	.00747	.00764	28
29	.00672	.00689	.00706	.00730	.00740	.00757	29
30	.00665	.00682	.00699	.00716	.00734	.00751	30
31	.00659	.00676	.00693	.00711	.00728	.00746	31
32	.00653	.00671	.00688	.00705	.00723	.00741	32
33	.00648	.00665	.00683	.00701	.00718	.00736	33
34	.00643	.00661	.00678	.00696	.00714	.00732	34
35	.00639	.00656	.00674	.00692	.00710	.00728	35
40	.00621	.00640	.00648	.00677	.00695	.00714	40
45	.00610	.00628	.00647	.00666	.00686	.00705	45
50	.00602	.00621	.00640	.00660	.00679	.00699	50

Mortgage Constant Table (Monthly Payments) (continued)

Years	8.50%	8.75%	9.00%	9.25%	9.50%	9.75%	Years
1	.08722	.08734	.08745	.08757	.08768	.08780	1
2	.04546	.04557	.04568	.04580	.04591	.04603	2
3	.03157	.03168	.03180	.03192	.03203	.03215	3
4	.02465	.02477	.02488	.02500	.02512	.02524	4
5	.02052	.02064	.02076	.02088	.02100	.02112	5
6	.01778	.01790	.01803	.01845	.01827	.01840	6
7	.01584	.01596	.01609	.01622	.01634	.01647	7
8	.01439	.01452	.01465	.01478	.01491	.01504	8
9	.01328	.01341	.01354	.01368	.01381	.01394	9
10	.01240	.01253	.01267	.01280	.01294	.01308	10
11	.01169	.01182	.01196	.01210	.01224	.01238	11
12	.01110	.01124	.01138	.01152	.01166	.01181	12
13	.01061	.01075	.01090	.01104	.01119	.01133	13
14	.01020	.01034	.01049	.01064	.01078	.01093	14
15	.00985	.00999	.01014	.01029	.01044	.01059	15
16	.00954	.00969	.00985	.01000	.01015	.01030	16
17	.00928	.00943	.00959	.00974	.00990	.01005	17
18	.00905	.00921	.00936	.00952	.00968	.00984	18
19	.00885	.00901	.00917	.00933	.00949	.00965	19
20	.00868	.00884	.00900	.00916	.00932	.00949	20
21	.00852	.00868	.00885	.00901	.00917	.00934	21
22	.00838	.00855	.00871	.00888	.00904	.00921	22
23	.00826	.00823	.00859	.00876	.00893	.00910	23
24	.00815	.00832	.00849	.00866	.00883	.00900	24
25	.00805	.00822	.00839	.00856	.00874	.00891	25
26	.00796	.00813	.00831	.00848	.00866	.00883	26
27	.00788	.00807	.00823	.00841	.00858	.00876	27
28	.00781	.00799	.00816	.00834	.00852	.00870	28
29	.00775	.00792	.00810	.00828	.00846	.00864	29
30	.00769	.00787	.00805	.00823	.00841	.00859	30
31	.00764	.00782	.00800	.00818	.00836	.00855	31
32	.00759	.00777	.00795	.00813	.00832	.00851	32
33	.00754	.00773	.00791	.00810	.00828	.00847	33
34	.00750	.00769	.00787	.00806	.00825	.00845	34
35	.00747	.00765	.00784	.00803	.00822	.00841	35
40	.00733	.00752	.00771	.00791	.00810	.00830	40
45	.00724	.00744	.00764	.00783	.00803	.00823	45
50	.00719	.00739	.00759	.00779	.00799	.00819	50

Mortgage Constant Table (Monthly Payments) (continued)

			Interest Rate				
Years	10.00%	10.25%	10.50%	10.75%	11.00%	11.25%	Years
1	.08792	.08803	.08815	.08827	.08838	.08850	1
2	.04614	.04626	.04638	.04649	.04661	.04672	2
3	.03227	.03238	.03250	.03262	.03774	.03286	3
4	.02536	.02548	.02560	.02572	.02585	.02597	4
5	.02125	.02137	.02149	.02162	.02174	.02187	5
6	.01853	.01865	.01878	.01891	.01903	.01916	6
7	.01660	.01673	.01686	.01699	.01712	.01725	7
8	.01517	.01531	.01544	.01557	.01571	.01584	8
9	.01408	.01421	.01435	.01449	.01468	.01476	9
10	.01322	.01335	.01349	.01363	.01378	.01392	10
11	.01252	.01266	.01280	.01295	.01309	.01324	11
12	.01195	.01210	.01224	.01239	.01254	.01268	12
13	.01148	.01163	.01178	.01192	.01208	.01223	13
14	.01108	.01123	.01138	.01154	.01169	.01185	14
15	.01075	.01090	.01105	.01121	.01137	.01152	15
16	.01046	.01062	.01077	.01093	.01109	.01125	16
17	.01021	.01037	.01053	.01069	.01085	.01102	17
18	.01000	.01016	.01032	.01049	.01065	.01082	18
19	.00981	.00998	.01014	.01031	.01047	.01064	19
20	.00965	.00982	.00998	.01015	.01032	.01049	20
21	.00951	.00968	.00985	.01002	.01019	.01036	21
22	.00938	.00955	.00973	.00990	.01007	.01025	22
23	.00927	.00944	.00969	.00979	.00997	.01015	23
24	.00917	.00935	.00952	.00970	.00988	.01006	24
25	.00909	.00926	.00944	.00962	.00980	.00998	25
26	.00901	.00919	.00937	.00955	.00973	.00991	26
27	.00894	.00912	.00930	.00949	.00967	.00985	27
28	.00888	.00906	.00925	.00943	.00961	.00980	28
29	.00882	.00901	.00919	.00938	.00957	.00975	29
30	.00878	.00896	.00915	.00933	.00952	.00971	30
31	.00873	.00892	.00911	.00930	.00948	.00968	31
32	.00869	.00888	.00907	.00926	.00945	.00964	32
33	.00866	.00885	.00904	.00923	.00942	.00961	33
34	.00863	.00882	.00901	.00920	.00939	.00959	34
35	.00860	.00879	.00898	.00918	.00937	.00956	35
40	.00849	.00869	.00889	.00908	.00928	.00948	40
45	.00843	.00863	.00883	.00903	.00923	.00944	45
50	.00839	.00859	.00880	.00900	.00921	.00941	50

Mortgage Constant Table (Monthly Payments) (continued)

Years	11.50%	11.75%	12.00%	12.50%	13.00%	13.50%	Years
			Interest Rate				
1	.08862	.08873	.08885	.08908	.08932	.08955	1
2	.04684	.04696	.04707	.04731	.04754	.04778	2
3	.03298	.03310	.03321	.03346	.03369	.03394	3
4	.02609	.02621	.02633	.02658	.02683	.02708	4
5	.02199	.02212	.02224	.02250	.02275	.02301	5
6	.01929	.01942	.01955	.01981	.02007	.02034	6
7	.01739	.01752	.01765	.01792	.01819	.01846	7
8	.01598	.01612	.01625	.01653	.01681	.01709	8
9	.01490	.01504	.01518	.01547	.01575	.01604	9
10	.01406	.01420	.01435	.01464	.01493	.01523	10
11	.01338	.01353	.01368	.01398	.01428	.01458	11
12	.01283	.01297	.01313	.01344	.01375	.01406	12
13	.01238	.01253	.01269	.01300	.01331	.01363	13
14	.01200	.01216	.01231	.01263	.01295	.01328	14
15	.01168	.01184	.01200	.01233	.01265	.01298	15
16	.01141	.01157	.01179	.01207	.01240	.01274	16
17	.01118	.01135	.01151	.01185	.01219	.01253	17
18	.01098	.01115	.01132	.01166	.01200	.01235	18
19	.01081	.01098	.01115	.01150	.01150	.01220	19
20	.01066	.01084	.01101	.01136	.01172	.01207	20
21	.01054	.01071	.01089	.01124	.01160	.01196	21
22	.01042	.01060	.01078	.01114	.01150	.01187	22
23	.01033	.01051	.01069	.01105	.01142	.01789	23
24	.01024	.01042	.01060	.01097	.01134	.01172	24
25	.01016	.01035	.01053	.01090	.01128	.01166	25
26	.01010	.01028	.01047	.01084	.01122	.01160	26
27	.01004	.01023	.01041	.01079	.01117	.01156	27
28	.00999	.01018	.01037	.01075	.01113	.01152	28
29	.00994	.01013	.01032	.01071	.01109	.01148	29
30	.00990	.01009	.01029	.01067	.01106	.01145	30
31	.00987	.01006	.01025	.01064	.01103	.01143	31
32	.00984	.01003	.01022	.01061	.01101	.01141	32
33	.00981	.01000	.01020	.01059	.01099	.01139	33
34	.00978	.00998	.01018	.01057	.01097	.01137	34
35	.00976	.00996	.01016	.01055	.01095	.01135	35
40	.00968	.00988	.01008	.01049	.01090	.01130	40
45	.00964	.00984	.01005	.01046	.01087	.01128	45
50	.00961	.00982	.01002	.01044	.01085	.01126	50

Mortgage Constant Table (Monthly Payments) (continued)

Years	14.00%	14.50%	Interest Rate 15.00%	15.50%	16.00%	16.50%	Years
1	.08979	.09002	.09026	.09049	.09073	.09097	1
2	.04801	.04825	.04849	.04872	.04896	.04920	2
3	.03418	.03442	.03467	.03491	.03516	.03540	3
4	.02733	.02758	.02783	.02808	.02834	.02860	4
5	.02327	.02353	.02379	.02405	.02432	.02458	5
6	.02061	.02087	.02115	.02142	.02169	.02197	6
7	.01874	.01902	.01930	.01958	.01986	.02015	7
8	.01737	.01766	.01795	.01824	.01853	.01883	8
9	.01633	.01663	.01692	.01722	.01753	.01783	9
10	.01553	.01583	.01613	.01644	.01675	.01706	10
11	.01489	.01520	.01551	.01582	.01614	.01646	11
12	.01437	.01469	.01501	.01533	.01566	.01599	12
13	.01395	.01428	.01460	.01493	.01527	.01560	13
14	.01360	.01394	.01427	.01461	.01495	.01529	14
15	.01332	.01366	.01400	.01434	.01469	.01504	15
16	.01308	.01342	.01377	.01412	.01447	.01483	16
17	.01287	.01322	.01358	.01394	.01429	.01465	17
18	.01270	.01306	.01342	.01378	.01414	.01451	18
19	.01256	.01292	.01328	.01365	.01402	.01439	19
20	.01244	.01280	.01317	.01354	.01391	.01429	20
21	.01233	.01270	.01307	.01345	.01382	.01420	21
22	.01224	.01261	.01299	.01337	.01375	.01413	22
23	.01216	.01254	.01292	.01330	.01369	.01407	23
24	.01210	.01248	.01286	.01325	.01363	.01403	24
25	.01204	.01242	.01281	.01320	.01359	.01398	25
26	.01199	.01238	.01276	.01316	.01355	.01395	26
27	.01195	.01234	.01273	.01312	.01352	.01392	27
28	.01191	.01230	.01270	.01309	.01349	.01389	28
29	.01188	.01227	.01267	.01307	.01347	.01387	29
30	.01185	.01225	.01264	.01305	.01345	.01385	30
31	.01182	.01222	.01262	.01302	.01343	.01384	31
32	.01180	.01220	.01261	.01301	.01342	.01382	32
33	.01179	.01219	.01259	.01300	.01340	.01381	33
34	.01177	.01217	.01258	.01299	.01339	.01381	34
35	.01176	.01216	.01257	.01298	.01338	.01379	35
40	.01171	.01212	.01253	.01294	.01336	.01377	40
45	.01169	.01210	.01252	.01293	.01334	.01376	45
50	.01168	.01209	.01251	.01292	.01334	.01375	50

Mortgage Constant Table (Monthly Payments) (continued)

Years	17.00%	17.50%	18.00%	18.50%	19.00%	19.50%	Years
			Interest Rate				
1	.09120	.09144	.09168	.09192	.09216	.09240	1
2	.04944	.04968	.04992	.05017	.05041	.05065	2
3	.03565	.03590	.03615	.03640	.03666	.03691	3
4	.02886	.02911	.02937	.02964	.02990	.03016	4
5	.02485	.02512	.02539	.02567	.02594	.02622	5
6	.02225	.02253	.02280	.02309	.02338	.02366	6
7	.02044	.02073	.02102	.02131	.02161	.02191	7
8	.01912	.01942	.01972	.02003	.02033	.02064	8
9	.01814	.01845	.01876	.01907	.01939	.01971	9
10	.01738	.01770	.01802	.01834	.01867	.01900	10
11	.01679	.01711	.01744	.01778	.01811	.01845	11
12	.01632	.01665	.01699	.01733	.01767	.01802	12
13	.01594	.01629	.01663	.01698	.01733	.01768	13
14	.01564	.01599	.01634	.01669	.01705	.01741	14
15	.01539	.01575	.01610	.01647	.01683	.01719	15
16	.01519	.01555	.01591	.01628	.01665	.01702	16
17	.01502	.01539	.01576	.01613	.01650	.01688	17
18	.01488	.01525	.01563	.01600	.01638	.01677	18
19	.01476	.01514	.01552	.01590	.01629	.01667	19
20	.01467	.01505	.01543	.01582	.01621	.01660	20
21	.01459	.01497	.01536	.01575	.01614	.01653	21
22	.01452	.01491	.01530	.01569	.01609	.01648	22
23	.01446	.01486	.01525	.01565	.01604	.01644	23
24	.01442	.01481	.01521	.01561	.01601	.01641	24
25	.01438	.01478	.01517	.01557	.01598	.01638	25
26	.01434	.01474	.01515	.01555	.01595	.01636	26
27	.01432	.01472	.01512	.01553	.01593	.01634	27
28	.01429	.01470	.01510	.01551	.01691	.01632	28
29	.01427	.01468	.01508	.01549	.01590	.01631	29
30	.01426	.01466	.01507	.01548	.01589	.01630	30
31	.01424	.01465	.01506	.01547	.01588	.01629	31
32	.01423	.01464	.01505	.01546	.01587	.01628	32
33	.01422	.01463	.01504	.01545	.01586	.01628	33
34	.01421	.01462	.01503	.01545	.01586	.01627	34
35	.01421	.01462	.01503	.01544	.01585	.01627	35
40	.01418	.01460	.01501	.01543	.01584	.01626	40
45	.01417	.01459	.01500	.01542	.01584	.01625	45
50	.01417	.01459	.01500	.01542	.01583	.01625	50

Tax Aspects of Apartment Ownership

"The thing generally raised on city land is taxes."

—CHARLES DUDLEY WARNER

Usually, taxation is about as enjoyable as a sore throat. However, for people who own apartment buildings, the tax system can provide some valuable advantages. In fact, to some investors, when purchasing an apartment property, tax benefits can be a significant motivating factor. This remains true even though the changes in the Tax Reform Act of 1986 eliminated some of the tax breaks previously available to owners of residential income property.

At this point, I want to give you a word of wisdom about offering tax advice to your clients: *DON'T!* While it is important for you to understand the tax aspects of apartment ownership, you should avoid counseling clients about taxation. This is a highly specialized field this is best handled by an experienced accountant.

The main reason we are dealing with taxation in this book is to help you learn enough about the subject to feel comfortable and self-confident when the conversation turns to the IRS and federal tax procedures.

Now, let's see how tax savings can add to the overall return on the investment in apartment buildings.

DEPRECIATION

Although an apartment building may be breaking even or providing cash flow on an operational basis, it can often produce a *loss* for income tax purposes because the Internal Revenue Code permits an owner to take a deduction from the building's income for depreciation.

Theoretically, a building loses part of its value every year because it is wearing out or becoming obsolete. The depreciation deduction is an allowance permitted by the IRS for this loss in value since the loss is essentially a cost of owning the property. However, the amount of depreciation deductions that an owner takes on his or her apartment building has little or no correlation to any variation in the property's worth. Indeed, the property is usually increasing in value even though the owner is taking a depreciation deduction.

Calculating the depreciation allowance for a specific building involves many factors. These include the allocation between land and improvements, the length of the depreciable life and the method of depreciation. If some of these terms look unfamiliar, you'll quickly understand them very clearly.

Allocation Between Land and Improvements.   The first step in calculating the depreciation allowance is to determine what percentage of the cost of the investment is depreciable. This is called the depreciable basis.

Only assets that wear out over time can be depreciated. Therefore, improvements are depreciable, but land is not. The allocation of the cost of the investment between land and improvements will be based on their relative fair market values.

Example: If an investor purchased a 12-unit apartment building for $500,000 and 70 percent of that cost was the fair market value of the improvements, he would be able to depreciate $350,000. ($500,000 × .70 = $350,000.)

Depreciable Life.   The depreciable life, also known at different times as the recovery period or useful life, is the number of years over which the depreciation allowance may be taken. For residential rental property the depreciable life is now set at 27.5 years for properties placed into service on or after January 1, 1987. The taxpayer may also choose, at his or her option, a 40-year depreciable life on a property-to-property basis. However, a shorter recovery period is usually more favorable to the investor because it allows larger annual depreciation deductions. Consequently, the investor gets the use of the money generated by the tax deduction at an earlier time.

Methods of Depreciation.   Methods of depreciation are formulas for spreading out the total available amount of depreciation deductions over the depreciable life. The use of accelerated depreciation was eliminated in the Tax Reform Act of 1986. Only the straight-line method of depreciation is now allowed in computing the depreciation deduction. Under this method the depreciable basis of the property is recovered proportionately over the allowable life.

In the above example, a building with a depreciable basis of $350,000 and a 27.5 year depreciable life would generate depreciation deductions of $12,727 a year for 27.5 years. The formula looks like this:

$$Depreciation\ Deduction = \frac{Depreciable\ Basis}{Depreciable\ Life}$$

This formula can also be expressed as a percentage rate. Just divide the depreciable life into 100 percent. The total value of the depreciable basis represents the 100 percent. Divide it by the current life of 27.5 years, and you're deducting 3.64 percent (rounded) of the depreciable basis annually.

TAXABLE INCOME AND AFTER-TAX CASH FLOW

In previous chapters we outlined in detail the method for determining gross income and subtracting vacancies and expenses to arrive at net income. We then deducted debt service to arrive at the pretax cash flow. Since the investor is most interested in cash flow after taxes, let's insert the depreciation deduction into the cash flow equation to determine the taxable income generated by the property and then proceed to calculate the after-tax cash flow.

Because a large portion of the value of an apartment property is depreciable, the application of the depreciation deduction will produce one of three consequences:

1. A portion of the cash flow from the property will be sheltered from taxes.
2. All of the cash flow from the property will be sheltered.
3. A sum larger than the cash flow from the property will be sheltered from taxes. When this is the case, the owner may be able to to use this "tax loss" to shelter income from other sources. However, there are limitations to the extent to which this can be done. (I'll explain in more detail below.)

Let's assume that our 12-unit apartment building produces an annual gross scheduled income of $61,200. If vacancy and expenses run 35 percent of the gross income and debt service is $31,592 a year ($300,000 loan at 10 percent interest for 30 yrs.), the pretax cash flow would be $8,188.

Gross scheduled income	$61,200
less expenses and vacancy (35%)	−21,420
Net operating income	39,780
less debt service	-31,592
Pretax cash flow	$ 8,188

The amount of pretax cash flow that is subject to taxation is determined by subtracting the annual mortgage interest (loan principal is not deductible) and depreciation deduction from the net operating income.

Net operating income	$39,780
less mortgage interest ($300,000 @ 10%)	-30,000
less depreciation deduction (see above)	-12,727
Taxable income	$(2,947)

In this example the entire pretax cash flow of $8,188 is sheltered from taxes. Since the taxable income is negative, the owner also has a "loss" of $2,947 that he *may* be able to use to shelter other income.

Before the Tax Reform Act of 1986, all such losses could be used to shelter income from other sources. However, the new laws now segregate income and losses into three categories: (1) active,

(2) passive and (3) portfolio. Wages, salaries, commissions and other income from personal services are classified as active income. Portfolio income consists of interest, dividends, annuities and royalties that are not derived during the ordinary course of a business. Income generated from the operation of rental property, regardless of the owner's level of activity in running the property, is regarded as passive income. Generally, for the purpose of determining the extent to which passive losses can be deducted, active and portfolio income may be grouped together.

The owner of income-producing real estate can only shelter active income with passive losses from rental properties in which he or she actively participates up to a maximum amount of $25,000. Active participation requires that the owner be involved, in a significant and bona fide way, in management decisions such as establishing rental rates, screening new tenants, and approving expenses for repairs and capital replacements. To qualify for the $25,000 allowance, the taxpayer must own at least ten percent of the property, and title cannot be held in the form of a limited partnership. Further, since the law was not intended to provide special benefits to the wealthy, the $25,000 maximum is reduced by an amount equal to 50 percent of the taxpayer's adjusted gross income over $100,000. Hence, he or she would lose all of the $25,000 write-off against active income once his or her adjusted gross income exceeded $150,000.

However, the taxpayer can continue to use passive losses to offset taxable income from other passive income sources without limitation in amount. For instance, an investor may own one rental property that is generating a positive taxable income of $40,000 and two others that are producing a combined tax loss of $30,000. He or she could then use the two figures to offset each other and reduce the taxable income from passive sources to only $10,000 ($40,000 − $30,000 = $10,000). Since an apartment investor's objective is to own properties that produce positive cash flows and neutral or negative taxable income, this aspect of the tax code should encourage owners of apartment buildings producing positive taxable income to purchase additional buildings under terms that will provide a tax loss. They can then use one property to shelter income from the other.

At this point, the final calculations needed to determine the after-tax cash flow of an apartment building are dependent on the owner's income tax rate. Because of tax reform, the multi-bracket graduated income tax rate schedule for individuals has been replaced with a two-bracket system.

Here is a breakdown of the new rate schedule as it will look when fully effective in 1988:

Single Taxable Income	Rate	Head of Household Taxable Income	Rate	Married Filing Jointly Taxable Income	Rate
$ 0–$17,850	15%	$ 0–$23,900	15%	$ 0–$29,750	15%
over 17,850	28%	over 23,900	28%	over 29,750	28%

As taxable income surpasses certain levels, the 15 percent bracket phases out and a 5 percent surcharge is imposed on income in the phaseout range. The consequence of the surcharge is that the effective marginal tax rate on income in the phaseout range is increased to 33 percent, creating a de facto third tax-rate bracket. The ranges for the phaseout are as follows:

> Single Taxpayers: $43,150 to $89,560
> Head of Household: $61,650 to $123,790
> Joint Returns: $71,900 to $149,250

The phaseout range for the 15 percent bracket and the separation points of the 15 percent and 28 percent brackets will be adjusted for inflation beginning in 1989.

We can now apply the owner's tax rate to the building's taxable income. If the taxable income is negative (as in our example), applying the tax rate will produce a tax savings for the owner. If the taxable income is positive, it will generate an additional tax liability. *Adding* the tax savings to or *subtracting* the tax liability from the before-tax cash flow results in the after-tax cash flow.

Assuming a 28 percent tax rate for the owner of the 12-unit building in our example, the property would produce a tax savings of $825 ($2,947 × .28 = $825 rounded). Adding the tax savings of $825 to the pretax cash flow of $8,188 produces an after-tax cash flow of $9,013.

TAX IMPLICATIONS UPON SALE

The sale of an apartment building is normally a taxable event. To determine the amount of tax liability generated by the sale, first calculate the taxable income or gain that the sale generates. To do this deduct any selling costs, that is, escrow and title fees, real estate commissions and so on, from the selling price to arrive at the amount realized. Then subtract the adjusted basis from the amount realized.

Taxable Income

Selling Price
− *Selling Costs*
= *Amount Realized*
− *Adjusted Basis*
= *Total Gain (Taxable Income)*

The adjusted basis is the original price paid for the property by the taxpayer plus the cost of any capital improvements less the amount of cumulative depreciation deductions taken.

For example, let's suppose our investor who purchased his or her 12-unit building for $500,000 held it for five years, made no capital improvements and took $63,000 in total depreciation deductions. The adjusted basis would be $437,000 ($500,000 − $63,000). In addition, he or she sells the property for $625,000 and incurs $40,000 in selling expenses. The amount realized is $585,000 ($625,000 − $40,000) and the difference between the amount realized and the adjusted basis is the total gain of $148,000 ($585,000 − $437,000).

Capital gains treatment was eliminated under the tax reform laws and gains from the sale of investment property are now taxed at the same rate as ordinary income. Applying the 28-percent tax rate to the gain of $148,000 gives the investor a tax liability of $41,440 from the sale of the property.

Taxes Due from Sale

Taxable Income (Total Gain)
× *Seller's Marginal Tax Rate*
= *Taxes Due from Sale*

TAX-DEFERRED EXCHANGES

An alternative to the usual rule requiring that gains or losses from the sale of real property be recognized is found in Section 1031 of the Internal Revenue Code. According to this section of the tax code, no gain or loss shall be recognized if property held for productive use in trade or business or for *investment* is *exchanged* solely for property of a like kind to be held either for productive use in trade or business or for investment. The words *like kind* refer to the nature or character of the property and not its grade or quality. Real property may be exchanged for real property as long as both meet the requirement of being held in trade or business or for investment. Obviously, exchanging one apartment building for another qualifies under the like-kind rule. An apartment building may even be exchanged for an office or industrial building. However, an apartment building cannot be exchanged for stocks, bonds or personal residence and qualify for tax treatment under Section 1031.

Exchanges under Section 1031 are variously referred to by real estate agents and investors as "tax-deferred," "tax-free" and "nontaxable" exchanges. Tax-free and nontaxable exchanges are misnomers because the seller's taxable gain is not forgiven in the exchange, but only deferred. And the deferral of taxes is the primary advantage to an owner from exchanging his or her property rather than selling it outright and reinvesting the proceeds.

To illustrate this point, consider an investor, who, by selling outright, incurs a tax liability of $75,000. Instead, if his intent were to sell and reinvest, by exchanging he would have retained the use of the $75,000 until the occurrence of a future taxable event, that is, until he sells outright. In essence, he is obtaining an interest-free loan from Uncle Sam for the duration of that period.

One important disadvantage of effecting a tax-deferred exchange is that the investor's basis in the property acquired is reduced by the amount of the gain that he or she is deferring. Since, as we have seen previously, the yearly and aggregate depreciation deductions are dependent on the taxpayer's basis in the property, an investor who obtains an apartment building in a tax-deferred exchange receives smaller annual depreciation deductions as well as smaller cumulative deductions than would be permitted in a purchase.

Example: An investor sold an apartment building for $700,000 net and had an adjusted basis at that time of $250,000. The seller reported a gain of $450,000 ($700,000 − $250,000) and was taxed at the ordinary income rate. If the investor then reinvested in another apartment building at a cost of $1 million, with improvements valued at $700,000 and land at $300,000, the basis in the property would be $1 million and he or she would be allowed to take $700,000 in depreciation deductions over 27.5 years for an annual deduction of $25,455.

However, if he or she exchanged the apartment complex for the new building, he or she need not report the gain of $450,000, but the basis in the new property would be only $550,000. The new basis is determined by adding the $250,000 basis of the old property plus $300,000 in "boot" needed to equalize equities (the $1 million price of the new property minus the $700,000 price of the old property equals $300,000). Further, he or she can only depreciate $385,000 (the 70-percent ratio of improvements to land times the $550,000 basis equals $385,000 depreciable basis) over the 27.5 year period. The end result is that the annual deduction for depreciation would be reduced to $14,000.

Because there are advantages and disadvantages to the use of the tax-deferred exchange, an investor must determine if he or she is better off paying the tax due on sale and then re-investing, or avoiding an immediate tax liability through a tax-deferred exchange. Advise your client that this decision is always best made with the help of competent legal and tax professionals.

Boot as mentioned in the above example is cash or other items given or received in addition to the property being exchanged. Boot can include stocks, bonds, notes or other personal property. When boot is involved in the exchange of property, you must note who is giving the boot and who is receiving it. For the investor giving the boot, as in the case above, the new basis of the property he acquires is the basis of the old property plus the amount of boot. For the investor receiving boot, a tax liability may be created by the exchange but limited only to the amount of the boot. Boot may also be received in the form of relief of indebtedness, which is treated as the receipt of cash. For instance, an investor may decide to exchange for a smaller property rather than a larger one. If he or she assumes a mortgage on the smaller property that is less than the mortgage amount secured by the property he or she is exchanging, the difference between the two mortgages is considered boot and is subject to taxation.

For simplicity of explanation, the above example involved a two-way exchange. However, in the course of your apartment sales career you will rarely find two investors willing to trade for each other's property. Most likely, you will encounter situations where one party wants to exchange property and the other wants to sell. In such cases, a third investor needs to be brought into the picture to create a three-way exchange.

Example: Investor A wants to exchange his apartment building for the one owned by B. However, B wants to sell his building and retire rather than exchange. Therefore, a third investor, C, must be found to purchase A's property. Investor A and investor B can exchange apartment buildings, and investor C then purchases A's former building from B.

In another approach, investor D, wishing to exchange, but not yet having located an exchange property, contracts to sell his building to buyer E with the provision that he be able to locate a suitable exchange property. The advantage here to D is that, with buyer E already in place to purchase his property, he will generally find it easier to negotiate a transaction with the owner of an exchange property once it is found. Any agreement between D and E should, however, state D's intention to restructure the transaction as a tax-deferred exchange within the meaning of Section 1031.

Normally, all properties involved in an exchange transaction would close concurrently. However, if E were unwilling to wait until D found an exchange property before purchasing D's building, D could close his deal with E and still create an exchange under the rules for a "delayed exchange." In such a scenario, D would be allowed 45 days to identify his exchange property after his closing with E and then would have an additional 180 days to close the transaction on the identified property.

Before you begin saying to yourself, "It is hard enough to get two investors to agree to a sale; how will I ever convince three to work together in an exchange?", let me assure you that it is done all the time.

You should, however, keep a couple of things in mind. While exchanges can be very rewarding—you have the opportunity to earn a commission for the purchase and sale of two properties—they can also be very time consuming. Throughout this book I stress the fact that the proper use of time can be your greatest asset in apartment sales, while the waste of it can be your biggest enemy. Therefore, be certain that you are dealing with motivated and qualified buyers and sellers who have realistic expectations of the marketplace. This certainty helps to ensure that the exchange will have a high probability of closing and that your investment in time will be adequately recompensed. (We will discuss ways to qualify buyers and sellers at great length in Chapters 7, 9 and 10.)

Also, until you obtain the experience and expertise necessary to guarantee that the obligations required for tax-deferred treatment are satisfied, limit your role in the exchange to finding a buyer for the investor's property, locating another property suitable for exchange, and negotiating the terms for the purchase and sale of each property. Since written agreements must be quite specific to secure the advantages of the tax-deferred exchange, have your client consult his or her attorney before he or she executes any agreements to acquire or dispose of property in an exchange.

INSTALLMENT SALES

Deferring taxes due upon the sale of an apartment building can also be accomplished through the utilization of an installment sale. Under this method of reporting capital gain, the sale is structured with the seller allowing the buyer to pay all or part of the purchase price over a number of years. The seller, in return, is permitted by the Internal Revenue Service to spread the gain over that period of time rather than having to report all of it in the year of sale.

Spreading the gain over time produces two main benefits to the seller of real property. The first is tax deferral. The taxes due on part of the gain are deferred until the buyer's installment payments are received by the seller. Consequently, the seller retains interest-free use of the tax liability that has been deferred until subsequent tax years. The second benefit is that spreading the gain over several years can help to keep the seller's taxable income from reaching higher income brackets. However, with the lower two-bracket system effective in 1988, this advantage may be mitigated for some investors.

Each payment under an installment sale consists of two parts. The first is the return of the investor's capital and the second is the amount of gain or profit. The amount of tax due on the total of all principal payments received in any given year is based on the percentage of the payment that is considered gain. The applicable percentage is known as the ''gross profit percentage.'' The gross profit percentage remains constant throughout the period that the obligation is outstanding and it is calculated using the following steps:

1. Determine the ''total gain'' by deducting selling expenses and the adjusted basis from the selling price.
2. Determine the ''total contract price'' by reducing the selling price by the lessor of (a) any qualifying indebtedness assumed or taken subject to by the buyer or (b) the selling price less selling expenses and adjusted basis. A qualifying indebtedness is a mortgage or other indebtedness encumbering the property that is assumed or taken subject to by the buyer.
3. Divide the total gain by the total contract price to find the gross profit percentage.

Example: Investor A sells an apartment building with an adjusted basis of $275,000 to Investor B for $500,000. A receives a $150,000 down payment and B assumes an existing mortgage of $200,000. A carries back the remaining $150,000 evidenced by B's promissory note secured by a mortgage against the property, amortized over 30 years with sufficient designated interest and payable in full in 5 years. A incurs selling expenses of $25,000. The total gain is $200,000 (selling price minus selling expenses and adjusted basis). The total contract price is $300,000 (selling price minus qualifying indebtedness). Therefore, the gross profit percentage is 67 percent ($200,000/$300,000). In the year of sale, 67 percent of the $150,000 down payment is reported as gain and 67 percent of all succeeding principal payments will be gain.

Situations can occur when an investor may want to report the entire gain from an installment sale in the year of sale. Those instances include circumstances in which the investor has sufficient tax loss to shelter the gain, when tax rates are expected to rise in subsequent years or because he or she has received comparatively little income during that year (including the gain from the sale).

As noted in the opening of this chapter, you're not expected to be a tax expert. But every bit of knowledge you can gain will increase your professionalism and your credibility with clients. And those are valuable assets to have in helping you sell apartment buildings and in putting big commission checks into your bank account.

Believe it or not, you are now ready to start creating apartment sales! In the next chapter, I'll show you how to put the marketplace right at your fingertips.

SUMMING UP WHAT YOU'VE LEARNED
IN CHAPTER 5

Although you should never act as a tax adviser to your clients, knowing how the tax code affects an apartment building investment enhances your status as a professional in the apartment sales field.

1. Even though an apartment building is breaking even or providing cash flow, it can often produce a *loss* for income tax purposes because of an allowance for depreciation.

2. Improvements are depreciable, but land is not. Therefore, for the purposes of determining the depreciation allowance, the cost of an apartment property is allocated between land and improvements.

3. The straight-line method of depreciation is the only method currently allowed to compute the depreciation deduction of an apartment building. The current depreciable life is 27.5 years.

4. The Tax Reform Act of 1986 limits the amount of "loss" from the operation of an apartment building that may be used to offset income from other sources.

5. Section 1031 of the IRS code gives a tax-deferred status to an exchange of "like kind" investment real estate, which delays the payment of taxes on the gain until an outright sale occurs in the future.

6. Boot is cash or other items given or received in addition to the property being exchanged in order to equalize the equities of the two properties.

7. Deferring taxes can be accomplished with an installment sale in which the seller allows the buyer to pay all or part of the purchase price over a number of years.

CHAPTER 6

Cataloging Your Territory

*"Nothing in this world can take
the place of persistence."*

—Calvin Coolidge

At football and baseball games usually a vendor walks through the crowd chanting, "You can't tell the players without a program." Likewise, in selling apartment buildings, you need to know the players—the sellers and buyers—and here's where a "program" comes in handy.

In this chapter, you'll learn how to build a roster of potential sellers by creating a catalog of apartment buildings that will literally put the marketplace at your fingertips. This catalog can be the most valuable tool you'll ever own because it will be your working guide to selling apartment properties.

I cannot emphasize too strongly the need to lay the groundwork for apartment sales very early in the game. Right now—before you get busy with actual selling—you have the time to put together the information you will need. In fact, starting on your apartment market catalog as soon as possible will actually hasten the day when you'll make your first big sale.

Because I created and use this catalog system myself, I can assure you that it works. Its main value is that it gives you the information you need to contact apartment owners directly and to *create sales opportunities where none had existed.* Just as the highest paying jobs usually are not listed in the "Help Wanted" ads, the most lucrative apartment sales possibilities normally are not found in the multiple listing service or in classified newspaper ads.

Cataloging apartment properties is the key to opening unlimited sales potential for you.

STARTING YOUR CATALOG

If you like playing detective, you'll really enjoy this easy method of compiling an inventory of possible sellers of apartment buildings. A three-ring binder, a camera, a current Thomas Brothers map book, some information sheets (such as the sample shown in Figure 6–1) and a couple of hours a day are all you need to begin your catalog system.

You probably already have chosen your market territory as discussed in Chapter 2. Now start your catalog by completing an information sheet with the following facts for every apartment building in your territory.

> Name of the building (if it has one)
> Address of the building
> Owner's name, address and phone number
> Number of units in the complex
> Date that the owner purchased the property
> Date you filled out the information sheet
> Photograph of the property
> (We'll deal with other data for the information
> sheet in subsequent chapters.)

You can use some of the same sources to find this information as you used in Chapter 2 to collect your comparable sales data.

Real Estate Data, Inc., for example, provides the addresses of apartment properties with the corresponding owner's name and address for most cities across the country. The property addresses are listed alphabetically by street on microfiche cards. This service makes it easy to gather information on buildings in the territory you've selected.

In some cities, companies exist that specialize in compiling this information in book form. One such firm in California is the Kurtz Publishing Company, 1815 South Pacific Avenue, Suite A, San Pedro, CA 90731. Their telephone number is 213-832-0354. If you live in another state, ask around in your real estate community to learn whether a service of this kind is available in your area.

Remember that title insurance companies can also be of great help to you. Check with your local title representatives to gather data on apartment buildings.

FIGURE 6–1

Building Name _____

Address _____

No. of Units _____ Date Acquired _____

Owner _____ Phone No. _____

Address _____ State _____ Zip _____

Date   *Comments*

_____

_____

_____

_____

_____

_____

_____

In most cases the sources I've mentioned will also be able to supply you with the date the owner purchased the property and the number of units in the complex.

If other people or services can't provide the information you need, or if you want to avoid any costs that may be involved, you can do the research yourself—an excellent way for you to get a firsthand acquaintance with buildings in your market.

Begin by driving up and down the streets of your territory and copying the addresses for all the apartment buildings you see. At the same time, you can estimate and write down the number of units in each complex. An exact figure is best, but if that is not obtainable, an approximation will do at this point.

Next, take the apartment addresses to the county tax assessor's office and search the public records to find the name of the owner and the address to which his or her property tax bill is sent; nine out of ten times this will be the home address. The assessor's office will probably also have the date the property was purchased. If not, you can look up the grant deed at the county recorder's office and note the date it was recorded.

Here's another tip. In this age of real estate syndication, you may find the ownership of a number of properties listed under the name of a partnership. However, when you contact the partnership, you'll want to know the names of the principal individuals involved. Fortunately, this information is easy to obtain. In most cases, the law requires partnerships to record a "partnership agreement" at the time they record their grant deeds. This partnership agreement contains the names of the principals. Since this agreement is a matter of public record, you can ask the county recorder to give you a copy.

FURTHER RESEARCH

The next step is to look up the telephone numbers of the building owners you are cataloging. As part of their services, one of the previously mentioned companies may already have listed the phone numbers for you. If not, you can look in many places in addition to the white pages of your telephone book.

People who have sufficient funds to invest in apartment buildings often are notable members of your community. As such, they often are listed, with a phone number where they can be reached, in directories of locally prominent people.

Contacts Influential International Corporation of Cleveland, Ohio, publishes business directories of this type for over 50 cities in the United States and Canada. You can write to this company at 20950 Center Ridge Road, Suite 106, Cleveland, OH 44116. The phone number is 216-333-6353.

Refer to such publications when the owner of a building has an unlisted phone number. Often you can find these owners listed as corporate executives, heads of civic organizations or chairpersons of charity fund-raisers. Calling one or more of these affiliations can probably lead you to the person who owns the apartment building you are researching.

A call to your local chamber of commerce will tell you if VIP phone lists are available in your community.

Another valuable source is the *AT&T Reverse Directory.* Instead of looking up a name, you simply check an address to find the telephone number used for that location. If you have a property owner's business address (a location other than the apartment building), that is all you need. Contact an AT&T office for more information about their reverse directories.

Remember, you can also take the direct approach that I mentioned in Chapter 2: Ask the apartment manager how you might contact the owner. This would seem the most obvious way to obtain a phone number, but in many cases apartment managers are instructed not to give out information about the ownership of the property. Still, this approach is worth a try.

If you cannot find an owner's phone number through these or any other sources you may come across, don't worry. I have devised a highly effective letter-writing campaign that I'll explain in Chapter 8.

USING PHOTOGRAPHS

In Chapter 2, I suggested that you take pictures of the apartment buildings that you visited during your rental survey. If you did that, you'll already have photos of some of the properties in your catalog. But you'll still need shots of all the other buildings that you have not yet visited, so here are some time-saving tips.

If you've been able to obtain a service such as Real Estate Data, Inc., to find apartment addresses and ownership records, the next step is to make a composite map of your selected sales territory. You can do that by cutting out segments from a Thomas Brothers map book or its equivalent in your area, and pasting the pieces together. Then, place a dot on the map for every apartment building location that you have in your catalog.

Now, using your map, plan the route you want to take to photograph the buildings shown by the dots on your composite map sheet. It makes sense to choose a route that will let you cover the most ground in the least time.

By planning your route carefully, you should be able to scan about 35 apartment buildings in an hour. Therefore, if you allow two to three hours for your trip, you will have photographed anywhere from 70 to 100 buildings in just one day.

If you do not have access to an apartment location publication, you'll want to photograph the buildings at the same time that you go out to scout their addresses.

I suggest that you use a compact, fully automatic aim-and-shoot camera, which you can purchase for around $100. With automatic focus and exposure features, motorized film advance and rewind, you can shoot fast and accurately from your car, without having to spend time focusing, reading meters and setting aperture and speed.

If you do use a manually set camera, follow the practice of professional photographers and bracket your shots. For example, if your meter tells you to shoot at 1/125 second with an aperture set at f/11, take one picture with that combination and then shoot a second picture at one stop larger (f/8) and a third picture at one stop smaller (f/16). Then you can select the best of the three prints. Bracketing shots is especially worthwhile on an overcast day or when photographing a light-colored building in glaring sunlight.

In any case, do not take a picture with a shutter speed of less than 1/60 of a second, and preferably at 1/125 or higher. Since you will be using a handheld camera rather than one on a tripod, higher shutter speeds provide sharp clear prints without the blurring caused by camera movement.

I recommend color print film with a speed of 100 ASA. This film is fast enough to cope with cloudy days and shadowed building areas and the grain is fine enough to give your pictures clear detail. I also suggest buying 36-exposure rolls because they cost less per shot and because you won't have to reload your camera as often as with smaller rolls.

When you plan your picture, be sure to include as much of the building as possible. The compact automatic cameras I suggested usually have a medium wide-angle lens, which is ideal for capturing a maximum view of the property.

Choose a camera angle that will include a street address so that you'll be able to match the picture with the appropriate information sheet for your catalog. If the apartment building is a large one, be sure to include the building's identification sign. The sign usually displays information such as the types of units in the complex, amenities (pool, dishwashers, and so on), perhaps the rental range and the phone number of the manager. That's considerable market information in one picture!

For each apartment building that you photograph, your goal is to make sure that you get enough information in your pictures to enable you to intelligently comment on the building when you speak to the owner by telephone. The owner will be pleased to hear you inquire about the "Colonial Arms" rather than "your apartment building." It won't do you any harm, either, to mention the beautiful landscaping or the red tile roof on the building. (We'll perfect your phone technique in Chapter 7.)

Here's another tip to help you collect as much property information as possible. Take along a battery operated, handheld tape recorder and dictate any pertinent facts about the property that your camera can't show with a single picture. You can later transfer these comments to your property information sheets.

Remember, the more knowledgeable and interested you appear, the more quickly you'll establish rapport with sellers and buyers. Note everything you can about the property. You are better off with a surplus of information than not enough.

I recommend that you have your film developed and printed the same day on which you shoot the pictures. One-hour developing and printing services cost more than processing that takes a week, but they are worth it. If you shoot your pictures early in the morning, you can drop off your film at a fast-service developer, take time for lunch and then pick up your prints. This way, your memory will still be fresh and you'll be able to quickly match the photos to the correct apartment information sheet in your catalog.

When you photograph the apartment buildings, take along your completed property information sheets, organized to correspond with your planned driving route. As you take each picture, write the number of the photo frame in the upper right-hand corner of the corresponding information sheet. After you have completed a roll of film, load another roll into your camera and number the pictures from that roll 1A, 2A, 3A and so on. Photos from successive rolls of film would be labeled 1B, 2B, 3B, then 1C, 2C, 3C, etc. Use a felt-tip pen to label the film canisters A, B, C and so on. (No need to label the first roll.) Ask the film developer to label the print envelopes the same way. With this simple system, you'll be sure that each building photograph corresponds to its correct property information sheet.

As you sort out your photos, paper clip or glue each one to the corresponding information sheet to be inserted in a three-ring binder. For ease of reference, organize the completed information sheets alphabetically by street name and then numerically by street address. Soon, you'll have a concise profile of each apartment building in your selected territory. You'll also want to add your tape recorded comments to the basic information, for example, "needs painting," "close to shopping," "quiet neighborhood, mostly adults" or any other points to remember.

As you expand your sales territory, your catalog will grow rapidly. For that reason, it's a good idea to use separate binders for each sector of your territory. If a prospective buyer asks about an apartment building in a specific area, you can quickly reach for the catalog binder for that region. Imagine how powerful a selling tool this will be when you bring a potential investor into your office and say, "Here's every apartment building in the area. Pick out the ones that interest you and I'll call the owner to see if he'll sell."

In very little time, you will have a catalog reference for hundreds, perhaps thousands, of apartment buildings, depending on the size of your market. Once the basic work is completed, all you'll need to do is to update individual pages as changes occur—a sale, upgrading of the property, newly constructed buildings in the area and other pertinent factors of interest to buyers.

Your catalog is an extremely important part of the selling techniques that can bring you a large and growing income. It's a proven way of putting market information right into your hands so that you can speak authoritatively about vast numbers of apartment buildings. Besides underscoring your credibility and stature as a specialist in the apartment sales field, possessing large amounts of accurate and current knowledge will give you a tremendous degree of self-confidence and the satisfaction of a worthwhile achievement. Best of all, your catalog will help you put buyers and sellers together and put big dollars into your pocket. And I'll show you how to do that in the next chapter.

SUMMING UP WHAT YOU'VE LEARNED
IN CHAPTER 6

A catalog of apartment properties in your area literally puts sales opportunities at your fingertips. Your catalog will be the most valuable income source you'll ever own. Begin it at once, and keep it updated.

1. Fill out an information sheet for every apartment building in your territory. Each page should contain complete property ownership information as well as a picture of the building.

2. For addresses of apartment properties and owners, contact one of the specialized data sources listed in this chapter or research the information yourself through title insurance companies and your local county recorder's office.

3. When photographing buildings for your catalog, plan your route carefully, so you can cover 25 to 35 buildings in an hour.

4. Include the name of the apartment building and a street address in your pictures. Use a one-hour photo-processing service.

5. Organize your completed information sheets by street name and numerically by street address.

6. Use separate three-ring binders for each sector of your territory.

7. Keep updating your catalog pages as changes in ownership, property conditions or other pertinent events occur.

CHAPTER 7

Hot Sales Leads from Cold Calls

*''Just know your lines and don't
bump into the furniture.''*

—Spencer Tracy

Get ready to use your apartment catalog now, because here's where we start the matchmaking between sellers and buyers. Here's where we also break with tradition. All you need is your telephone.

In the usual real estate structure, people in the business are either listing agents or selling agents. Those who list properties generally sit around waiting for a friend or relative to decide to move to another residence. The agent will then finally have a listing to sell. Those who represent buyers check the properties listed by other agents and hope to find a listing that might be of interest to some unknown client who, they hope, will just happen to stroll into their real estate office.

This system is fine for people with unlimited patience, lots of time on their hands and no great desire to earn commissions. It's a passive sales situation that does not satisfy progressive individuals who want to enjoy a high income and personally rewarding real estate career.

As I've said before, with my plan you'll learn how to create sales opportunities where none seemed to exist, and you'll open your own doors to a steadily growing income. More good news: You'll often be both listing and selling agent, and that can mean earning both sides of the commission.

To build unlimited sales volume, you'll need to know how to make effective ''cold calls.'' While reading those words, you may be asking, "Who, me? Make cold calls?" Relax. In just a few minutes, you'll discover ways to overcome what is a common and needless problem.

To begin, if you suffer from "cold call-itis," you have lots of distinguished company. Every profession and business has its own mental blocks. Young doctors worry about their first patients pulling through. New attorneys can get stage fright before their first court performances. And for salespeople, making the first cold calls can seem like signing on as a crew member of the Titanic.

If you're presently in real estate, you probably went through that ordeal under fire known as "farming." If you don't have a real estate background, you don't know what you've missed. Farming is a diabolical endurance test in which you knock on strange doors in strange neighborhoods, introduce yourself to even stranger people and ask to list their houses for sale. Their answer is usually NO because (a) they have a brother who's in real estate; (b) they are going to advertise their house "for sale by owner"; (c) you interrupted them during their favorite TV program or (d) something equally important.

If you've tried phoning people whom you don't know, you probably ended up talking to someone who wanted to know how much the neighbors down the street got for their house, or you talked with the silent type who abruptly ended your side of the conversation with a click and a dial tone.

The reason I've pointed to some pitfalls of contacting prospects with conventional methods is that they are exactly that: *conventional* methods. But I am showing you *unconventional* approaches to selling apartments with techniques that work. As I stated at the beginning of this book, all you have to do is follow my proven techniques. Sales will follow your efforts.

Right here, let's clear away an obstacle—the mental blocks that can trip up unwary salespeople. The key word is *mental*. The only person who can put rocks in your path is *you*. No one is trying to bar you from making a sale. No one is out to halt your progress. Remember that famous line from the Pogo comic strip? "We have met the enemy and they are us." Therein lies both the problem and the solution.

You ought to be glad that any obstacle to your success is within your own mind because you can eliminate it. The power to create a problem is also the power to do away with it. If obstacles to your progress were within someone else, you couldn't do a thing about it.

I can promise you that you will make cold calls easily with my method, and you will easily make them pay off—both in commissions and in a strong sure sense of self-confidence that can help you reach any goal you set for yourself.

If you're hesitant about making cold calls, changing one word can make all the difference. In your mind, replace *selling* with *telling*. Think about it. If I were to ask you to *sell* something— say, a sports car—to someone, you'd feel forced to make the sale. However, if I asked you to *tell* someone about that same car, you'd have no difficulty at all in praising that sporty set of wheels. In fact, you'd probably be so enthusiastic you'd very likely make a sale almost without knowing it.

To twist an old phrase, it's a matter of mind over chatter. *What* you say is critically important and it's especially important for *you* to control the cold-call conversation.

Let's get into some actual examples.

The first step in putting buyers and sellers together is to develop a roster of *qualified* buyers who are ready to purchase an apartment building that meets their investment requirements. ''Where do I find these buyers?'' you wonder. The answer is in the comparable sales data you learned about in Chapter 2.

First, remember that apartment buyers are primarily real estate *investors*—people who buy and sell apartments like any other commodity on the open market. Chances are, if they already own an apartment building or have just sold one, they could be seeking to purchase another. Therefore, you'll want to check your comparable sales data sources to compile a list of people who have bought or sold apartment properties in the recent past.

The next step is to phone these investors and see if they are looking for additional apartment properties. Your phone call should go something like this:

Mrs. Jackson, my name is John Sales with Associated Apartment Brokers, and I specialize in marketing apartment properties. I've noticed that a couple of years ago you purchased the Remington Manor Apartments on Essex Avenue. I'm always searching for good apartment investments for my clients, and I wanted to know

if you would be interested in acquiring another apartment building if a good opportunity presents itself.

In the case of a recent seller, you could easily modify the conversation to fit the situation.

Mrs. Jackson, my name is John Sales with Associated Apartment
Brokers. I'm a real estate agent specializing in the sale of apartment properties and I noticed that a few months ago you *sold* your
Remington Manor Apartments on Essex Avenue. I'm calling to
see if you intend to reinvest the proceeds from that sale into
another apartment building.

You could easily strike a responsive note with that first phone
call because apartment building investors are usually on the look-
out for another property. Our Mrs. Jackson, for example, may
want to add another building to her holdings. Or she may want
to dispose of her present apartment building and buy a larger
one to obtain more leverage or better tax benefits. (What a great
possibility for you to earn *two* commissions—one for selling her
a different apartment property and a second commission for selling her present building!)

Cold calls to prospective buyers also have another practical purpose, and that is to *prequalify* buyers. Your most important asset
is time, and you can't afford to waste endless hours and days
with unqualified would-be buyers who have unrealistic perceptions of the marketplace. Every marketing garden has a few
weeds, and it's better to pull them out of your prospect lists as
soon as you are aware of them.

On the positive side, when you contact serious prospective
buyers, you'll want to obtain specific information from them that
will help you zero in on the type of building they're looking for.

When you find an investor interested in buying additional
properties, continue the phone conversation by asking how many
units he or she is interested in purchasing and how much capital he or she has available. The answers to these important questions will help you quickly determine the prospective buyer's
needs and capabilities.

If, for example, your prospect has $100,000 cash and 25 per-
cent down is the prevailing amount of leverage used in the
marketplace, you know that he or she can afford a building with

a sale price of up to $400,000. If you use the price-per-unit method of calculating apartment values, based on a hypothetical $40,000 per unit, you also know that this particular prospect can buy a property with approximately ten units.

Determining the price and unit number categories automatically leads you to the most appropriate properties in your catalog system. These figures also let you know if your buyer's expectations are realistic. If your prospect hopes to buy a 25-unit complex with $100,000 capital, you obviously will have to educate him or her about the facts of the real estate market in your area. Never be timid about presenting the facts regarding the apartment market. Your prospect will respect you for knowing the truth and telling it honestly. Better yet, your prospect will probably *want* to be your client.

Ask, too, whether your prospect prefers "pride of ownership" properties or "fixer-uppers." Are there specific areas in which he would like to buy? Answers to questions like these will help you further pinpoint those buildings that will be of interest.

The final prequalifying question to your prospective buyer should be, "If I find the property you want, at a fair price, are you willing to purchase that building at this time?" If the answer is a definite yes, you have a good chance for a potential sale. If the answer is no, tell your prospect you'll keep in touch. Then, start talking to more likely buyers.

If you feel confident that you've found a motivated and qualified prospect, the next step is to set up an appointment to introduce yourself in person. Using my cold-call method, you could say, "Mrs. Jackson, could I have just a few minutes of your time? I'd like to meet you personally and show you some exciting possibilities. I cover the apartment market very thoroughly and can tell you about some specific properties that may be of interest to you." I can hear you thinking, "But I don't have any properties to show her." Yes you do. You'll have every apartment building in your catalog to show her! Earlier, I said that the best deals are often the ones that are not on the market. If our Mrs. Jackson sees a property in your catalog that interests her, you can call the owners of the building to see if they are willing to sell. See what's happening? You are beginning to create sales opportunities where none had existed. (I'll show you how to approach the potential seller of a property in a moment, but first, let's finish our discussion of the buyer.)

Now it's time to use the professional salesperson's technique for making an appointment. Rather than asking, "When could I see you?" give your prospect a choice of dates. "Would the end of this week or the early part of next week be more convenient for you, Mrs. Jackson?" you ask. Given alternatives, people usually feel compelled to make a choice. Expecting the buyer to name a meeting date generally results in a vague suggestion about getting together sometime in the future, which never comes. If the owner prefers the end of the week, for instance, suggest Thursday or Friday and ask for a morning or afternoon preference. Now, you have a specific appointment for, say, 10:00 A.M. on Thursday.

When you guide the appointment setting, you are also starting to control the situation, a very important factor as mentioned earlier.

If your prospect agrees to an appointment, try to steer the meeting place to your office by saying:

> I'll be happy to visit you at your address, but I also welcome you to my office. I have a large file of apartment ownership data, including pictures of all of the apartment buildings in the area. If you see any that you like, I'll call the owners to see if they will sell.

Having the buyer come to your office is a decided advantage for you because you'll be able to overwhelm him or her with your extensive catalog of apartment properties. This way, you'll not only be covering considerable ground in a short time, you also will be establishing yourself as an authority in your local apartment market. However, if a prospect wants the first meeting to be in his or her office, that's a good starting point too. You can always take along one of your catalog books and show the prospect the system you will use to find the best possible property for his or her needs.

Several important items should be discussed at the meeting with your potential purchaser. In general, you'll want to learn as much about the buyer as you can. You'll want to elaborate on the questions that you posed during your phone conversation, detailing locations and types of apartment properties that the buyer is interested in pursuing. You'll also want to know his or her motivation for buying an apartment building. An investor purchases apartment properties for three main reasons: for income, appreciation and tax shelter. Knowing his or her invest- ment motives will help you further zero in on appropriate proper- ties for a particular buyer. If a buyer is purchasing strictly for tax shelter, for example, you may want to concentrate your efforts on buildings that have a high ratio of improvements to land value. However, if the investor is buying solely for appreciation, you may want to look for a property that can be bought with a high degree of leverage. For the client who wants income, a smaller property with a large down payment may be the best answer.

You'll also want to know if the buyer's capital is readily avail- able. By readily available, I refer to capital that is in a highly liquid form such as a savings account, money market or certificate of deposit. If the buyers need to refinance or sell another property to generate the cash necessary for the down payment, you should instruct them to start that process immediately so that funds will be available when you find the right apartment building for them. Naturally, if they want to sell or exchange another apartment building, you'll tell them that you're the real estate agent they need to handle that transaction.

It's important to be working with buyers whose capital is readily accessible. When you present an offer to a seller, he or she will be concerned about the buyer's ability to perform. Your job of getting the offer accepted will be much easier when you can tell the seller that you have a qualified buyer who is in a posi- tion to close the deal as soon as all contingencies have been removed. (We'll discuss contingencies in a later chapter.)

Ultimately, you'll want to acquire enough buyers so that you'll have a potential investor for every size and type of apartment building in your territory. However, you'll be ready to start calling sellers as soon as you have found your first investor client.

MEET THE OTHER TEAM

It's time now to turn our attention to the other players in the apartment brokerage game: the sellers.

With your list of potential buyers in hand, open your catalog to the buildings that fit their requirements and start making phone calls to apartment owners. Your first contact is Mr. Robert Wilson, who owns an 18-unit apartment building. Your side of the conversation should be something like this:

> Hello, Mr. Wilson. This is John Sales of Associated Apartment Brokers. I'm a real estate agent specializing in the sale of apartment properties. I represent a buyer with a substantial amount of cash who's looking for 15 to 20 units in the Ridge Crest area and I think your Armstrong Court Apartments on Hilltop Drive could be of interest to my buyer. I am calling to see if you would entertain an offer to sell your property.

Compare this approach with the usual phone inquiry that says, "I'm Fred Guesser of Hopeful Realty and I was wondering if you'd like to sell your apartment building."

What is the problem with the latter approach, the conventional one? Everything—because the caller has told the apartment owner virtually nothing of value. This kind of phone call will probably get a negative response, not because the owner doesn't want to sell, but because he or she hasn't been given any *reasons* to consider a sale.

Now, look at the advantages of the first technique, the one I have used successfully hundreds of times.

In less than thirty seconds, the caller has told the building owner: (1) who he is and the name of his company; (2) that he is a specialist in the apartment market; (3) that he has a possible buyer with cash; (4) that the buyer is looking for a specific size apartment property (Note that we said "15 to 20 units" in this example. It's best to bracket the number of units in the owner's building so that the approach doesn't sound too contrived.); (5) that he is familiar with the name and location of the owner's property and (6) that a purchase offer may be in the making.

Please note the phrase "entertain an offer" in the recommended approach. Again, here is where words are extremely important. You must make the property owner comfortable with your introductory phone call. That's why you are asking him or her merely to *entertain* an offer—to think about it, consider it, mull it over. No pressure, no heavy pitch.

In this call you are not doing any selling at all. You are *telling* an apartment owner about an intriguing possibility: making money by selling his property. You have sparked interest and curiosity and, at the same time, you have established credibility for yourself—a tremendous asset.

To test the validity of this approach, put yourself in the place of the property owner. Wouldn't *you* be interested in at least talking further about a possible sale if it meant a generous profit for you?

To make an appropriate offer, your buyer will need to know the unit mix, rent schedule, financing and all other pertinent facts concerning the building. To get the necessary data, the next step is to set up a meeting with the apartment owner who shows a willingness to "entertain" a purchase offer. (I'll give you some tips on how to conduct that meeting in Chapter 9.) All you need do in this example is to extend your opening phone call as follows:

> Mr. Wilson, in order to make an intelligent offer for your building, my buyer will need additional information concerning your property. I'd like to stop by for a few minutes of your time, meet you and fill out an information sheet on your property. Would the end of this week or the early part of next week be more convenient for you?

You can then go on to nail down the appointment for a specific day and time.

You may be asking, "Why can't I just get the information over the phone?" If you can't set up an appointment with the owner, gathering information by phone is better than not getting it at all. However, keep in mind that the *main* purpose of this first phone call is to arrange a visit with the owner *in person*. The sooner you have face-to-face meetings with prospective sellers and buyers, the faster you can develop the bond of trust and confidence needed between broker and client to successfully transact an apartment sale.

It is true that not every apartment owner is going to be ready to sell the first time you call. However, remember that existing property owners are a prime source of potential *buyers*. Therefore, if an owner tells you he is not interested in selling at the time you call, use the following approach to learn if he's interested in *buying:*

> Mr. Wilson, are you interested in acquiring additional property at this time? I'm constantly in touch with owners like yourself,

and I'd be happy to call you right away when I come across a property that fits your investment needs.

If you get a positive response, continue in the same manner we discussed earlier to qualify him and make an appointment to meet with him in person.

It is also true that most owners *do* sell at some point. Timing is an important part of your success as an apartment salesperson. Be sure to schedule future phone calls as follow-ups. For instance, if a property owner doesn't have immediate plans to sell or buy, keep your contact alive by inquiring about the possibility of a meeting later on. You can do this by asking, "Mr. Wilson, even though you may not have definite plans to buy or sell right now, would there be a good time for me to call you again in the future?" Mr. Wilson may tell you that he intends to retire in two years and has considered selling his property at that time. Or he may want to sell his apartments after the first of the year for tax purposes. He may even tell you he owns *another* apartment building (one that you didn't even know about) that he is willing to sell soon. Good questions on your part can often turn up happy surprises!

If all this sounds easy, it is—in most cases, at least.

However, we both know that we don't live in a fairy-tale world in which our sales prospects always say yes to whatever we suggest. If that were true, we'd all become millionaires without really trying, and you wouldn't be reading this book.

Let's look at some roadblocks and ways to get around them when you make cold calls to apartment owners.

TURNING NEGATIVES INTO POSITIVES

Here are some general points to keep in mind about the potential seller who says no the first time you talk to him or her.

If you get an initial turndown, it may simply be because the person doesn't know you. He or she may also be wary about being taken advantage of or may fear a high-pressure pitch. Therefore, don't abandon the call too quickly. Try to continue the conversation by diplomatically ignoring the objection and probing for ways to warm up the owner.

Here's where it helps to show a personal interest in the property. Remember the picture you took of the building for your catalog? You can now use it to good advantage by saying, "That's a great color for your building. Did you select it?" Everyone has an ego, and complimenting the property is a good way to generate further conversation.

Maybe you'll mention the attractive landscaping or how well the property is maintained (if those are valid observations). The point is simply to elicit enough of a friendly response to keep the conversation moving toward arranging a personal meeting.

Above all, *never* say anything that will put you and the owner in an adversarial position. For instance, if the apartment owner says he or she isn't interested in entertaining an offer to sell, a deadly mistake is to bluntly ask, "Why not?" That's like pulling the pin on a hand grenade. No one likes to have his or her judgment pointedly questioned, especially by a stranger. However, it is important to try to ascertain the *reason* for the negative response. Once you've found out why the owner is not interested in selling, you may be able to overcome the objections and give some reasons why he or she might consider selling. The best way to do that is to ask an important preliminary question: "Mr. Jackson, would it be alright if I asked you a couple of additional questions?" The strategy, of course, is that by requesting the owner's permission to ask further questions, you are taking the heat off yourself. At the same time, you are gently rolling the ball into your prospect's court, and he or she will very likely be willing to answer your queries.

When the conversation continues, you can feel free to ask directly, "Is there a particular reason why you haven't thought about selling your building?" Notice that I avoided asking for "the reason why you've *decided* not to sell your building." Psychologically, you weaken your position when you suggest that the owner may have reached a decision not to sell. Asking why the owner hasn't *thought* about selling is much more flexible and leaves the door open for the owner to consider reasons *for* selling.

With those basic points in mind, here is a list of objections you might encounter and proven ways to overcome them.

"I can't sell because of my tax situation." With this owner, you can suggest the benefits of an installment sale or exchange for a larger property. Tell him you'd like to meet with him and dis-

cuss ways in which your buyer would be willing to structure the sale to help improve his tax advantages.

"My building is doing fine and I plan to keep it." Point out the fact that a building with low vacancy rates commands the best price. If the market turns downward, too many empty units could make the building hard to sell. Suggest a meeting to show the owner the price you think your buyer would be willing to pay for the property.

"My rents are too low and I'd take a beating if I sold now." Here is an ideal opportunity for you to tell this owner about the rental survey you've conducted. Offer to meet with him to show him where his rents should be. (Everyone appreciates free information.) Depending on market conditions, you could report that you have a buyer who would pay a fair price for the building with rents remaining at current levels. You can also further qualify the owner by asking if he would sell if rents were at prevailing market levels.

"I think the market isn't right at the present time." Express interest in his viewpoint and ask why he believes market conditions are not favorable. (Most people like to expound on their theories.) When he gives you his reply, you may be able to change his perceptions of the marketplace. And, if you have recently sold an apartment property near his, tell him about the transaction and ask to meet with him to show him what price he can expect to get for his building.

"Maybe I'll sell in a few months. Call me later on." Diplomatically counter this response by asking the owner if there is a specific reason why he is postponing selling his building. Remind him that a sale transaction takes time, and that you can structure a sale that will close at about the time he plans to sell. If he firmly doesn't want to sell until a later date, take down the information and then call him a few weeks before the date he suggests.

"I'm interested in selling. I'll send you the information about my property." This reply is close to "I'll put the check in the mail." Don't count on it. Tell the owner you'll be glad to pick up the

property information to save his time. Mention, too, that it will take only a few minutes to review the data with him.

"Sell my apartments? What for?" Take your choice of a number of good answers to that question: If the market is strong, tell him that right now is the best time to get a good price for his building. Remind him that selling frees him from the hassles of managing apartments. Maybe he's near retirement age. Suggest that he sell now, take the money and do the things he has always wanted to do. Ask him to consider selling for estate planning purposes. Or suggest trading for a larger or smaller building, depending on his needs.

"Why do I need a broker? I can sell my building myself." Inform this owner that you are a specialist in selling apartments. As such, you can get him top dollar for his property and probably net him the same amount as if he sold it himself. Remind him that his time is valuable and he can best use it by doing what he does best, while allowing you to help him by doing what you do best.

"I'm really too busy to meet with you now. Call me back in about a month." Explain, "I need only a few minutes of your time. I have a qualified buyer who would be interested in making an offer on your building." If this owner still says he's too busy, qualify him by asking, "Will you be available in a month?" If he says yes, call back in two weeks.

"I just sold my building." Don't give up. Ask if the sale has closed yet. If not, keep in touch with the seller on a weekly basis. Transactions often fall apart. Be ready. Find out the sale price, terms and any other details of the sale you can elicit from the owner. If the transaction has closed, get all the pertinent facts for your comparable sales data. Be sure to ask if the owner has other property to sell, and inquire how he plans to reinvest the proceeds from this sale. You could come up with a client after all!

The preceding examples obviously do not cover every possible scenario, but they do illustrate the necessity for you to keep probing for opportunities to meet with apartment owners who give a negative response during your phone contacts with them.

FOLLOW-UP CALLS

At this point, let me emphasize the importance of keeping track of your phone calls to apartment owners. Note the time and date of your phone contact in the comments section on the corresponding catalog sheet. Also jot down any pertinent facts you learned in the phone conversation. Then call back in six months. To make sure you will remember to call a half-year later, mark the owner's name and phone number on the proper future date on your calendar. In fact, you should call back your prospects *at least* every six months.

Keep in touch with your prospects because their plans can and do change. A divorce, a death in the family, a destructive tenant or a broken water pipe in the middle of the night can cause an "I-won't-sell" owner to suddenly want to put the property on the market.

Never believe an owner who says "never." I learned that lesson the hard way. When I was less experienced, an apartment owner told me that he would *never* sell his building. I took his word for it and gave up on him as a prospect. Six months later, a friend of his suffered a severe heart attack, and, fearing the same thing might happen to him, the apartment owner sold everything he possessed and set out to travel and have fun. Because I failed to keep in touch with this owner, another agent got the sale.

When you do phone an owner you called about six months before, here's an effective approach based on sound strong psychology: "Mr. Wilson, this is John Sales. How have you been? (Pause.)"

Let's use that brief pause to consider the strategy here. Although Mr. Wilson may not remember who you are, everyone appreciates someone showing interest in his well-being. With your first sentence you're warming up the owner and creating the atmosphere necessary for further conversation. Then, you continue:

> I'm with Associated Apartment Brokers. I spoke to you about six months ago regarding your Armstrong Court Apartments in the Ridge Crest area. At the time, you said you weren't interested in selling, but I wanted to get back to you because I still have a buyer interested in purchasing 15 to 20 units in your area. I wanted to

know if you would entertain an offer to purchase your building at present.

If you get a green light with this follow-up call, immediately set up an appointment using the method you learned earlier in this chapter.

As you talk with prospective sellers and buyers, feel totally free to handle the conversation in your own style. The examples I've given you are intended only as guidelines that incorporate certain elements that have proved effective. I wrote the music, so to speak, but you'll be the one to play the tune. Be yourself. The only cautionary reminder I would give you is that honesty is still the best policy. Telling an apartment owner you have a buyer when none exists is dangerous in more ways than one. Protect your integrity and credibility at all times because those two qualities are the most important foundations of your career.

No phone call to a prospective seller or buyer is ever wasted. Every time you phone prospects, your name becomes more familiar to them. At some time in the future, they are going to contact someone about an apartment transaction, and you want that someone to be *you*.

DEVELOPING COLD-CALL SKILLS

Here's where talking to yourself pays.

To develop your cold-call technique (when you're alone in your office or home), pretend you're talking to an apartment owner— with no one at the other end of the phone line. Practice introducing yourself to your imaginary phone conversation partner. Ask questions. Set up an appointment. Mention your catalog of apartment properties. Add anything else you think might be of interest to an apartment owner. Thank the person you "called" and think over your part of the conversation. Then try another make-believe call, this time to an owner who swears he will never never sell. How do you handle that situation? How can you do better the next time?

Better yet, if you're working in a real estate office where other agents are also selling apartments, get together and practice *role playing*. One of you assumes the role of the agent and the others the roles of the potential buyer and seller. Create phone conversations between the players that will help you improve your skills or overcome any particular problems you may be having in your cold-calling technique.

If you have a tape recorder, actually hearing your telephone technique is another good way to test how well you're doing your cold calling. When you play back your voice, you'll quickly spot the areas where you need improvement. But don't be too hard on yourself. Above all, don't be afraid to make mistakes—even in phone calls to actual people. Your phone performance will improve rapidly and you'll soon be cold calling like a seasoned pro.

TELEPHONE TIPS

Here are some tested proven guidelines for using the phone most effectively for making cold calls.

1. **Make sure you're calling at a favorable time.** After you introduce yourself, if you suspect you may have called at the wrong time, ask your prospect if you're interrupting him or her in something important. When you use the word *important*, people usually will be willing to listen. On the other hand, if you are really disturbing them while they're busy, they will appreciate your offering to call back at a later time.

2. **Talk to the top banana.** If the owner or the chief principal of an apartment property is not available when you phone, don't waste your time talking to a relative or resident manager. If the person answering the phone suggests you talk to anyone less than the main decision maker, politely state that you really must speak with the owner. Ask when that individual will be available and call again. Never leave a message about the reason for your call. You know what they say about words losing something in translation.

3. **Use your best voice.** When you phone a prospect for the first time, *your phone voice is you*. Because that initial impression is vitally important, be sure to speak in a cordial easy tone of voice. Picture your prospect really enjoying hearing from you because you may be bringing him good news. If you feel tense, you'll *sound* tense. Relax. Visualize lolling on a Hawaiian beach, sailing along on gently rolling waves or whatever seems especially pleas-

ant to you. Here is where your tape recorder can help you smooth out your style and develop a friendly upbeat tone of voice. Practice and listen, practice and listen.

4. **Not too fast, not too slow.** If you deliver your phone message at jet speed, you'll jar your prospect and may even cause him to suspect that he is literally getting a "fast pitch." Talking too rapidly also can cause you to garble some words. On the other hand, talking too slowly can give your prospect the impression that you're not sure of yourself and can also make the person start looking at his or her watch. Speak at a normal rate, the way you do when you are having a casual conversation with a friend. Remember, the whole idea of the cold call is make your prospect feel comfortable with you and to look forward to meeting you.

5. **Be a good listener.** If you've heard that advice a thousand times, it's because we all need to remind ourselves to truly *hear* what another person is saying. I have witnessed many agents actually talk a possible sale out of existence. Don't laugh. It happens too frequently. Some salespeople are so involved in what they are trying to say, they do not listen to what a prospect is telling them. It's an easy mistake to make, and a very costly one—both in cold calling by phone and, of course, in personal meetings.

6. **Be flexible.** Constantly adapt your end of the phone conversation to what your prospect is telling you about his or her situation. The faster you can think on your feet, the sooner you'll turn a prospect into a client. What's the magic word again? You've got it: practice.

7. **Don't tell it all on the phone.** If a novel revealed the whole story plot in the first paragraph, you'd probably never read the entire book. The same thing applies to cold calling. Be complete enough so that your prospect knows who you are and why you're calling. But leave the main part of your story (your rental survey, comparable sales data, and your catalog information) for your face-to-face meeting. That is why you are making your cold calls in the first place.

SET YOUR GOALS AND TIME SCHEDULE

No one has ever realized a large and worthwhile reward without setting and following goals. Because cold calling is so essential to building your apartment sales career, establishing how many calls you'll make each week and at what times is extremely important.

Two major reasons exist for faithfully adhering to a firm schedule for cold calling. First—and obviously—the more phone calls you make, the better your chances for success. Second, cold calling must be an ongoing process because there's often a sizable time period between your initial contact with a prospect and the closing of the transaction. If you don't continue making cold calls while you're putting together a certain deal, you'll miss future sales opportunities you should be developing as you go along. Think of your business as a pipeline. To keep sales flowing out one end, you must keep pouring cold calls into the other end.

How many cold-call contacts you make each week is up to you. Remember, the only thing that counts is the number of *appointments* you obtain. I've found it productive to keep a steady goal of making at least *two appointments each week*. At first, you may make 30 to 40 phone calls to secure two meetings with prospects. Later, as your technique improves, you may get those two (or three or four) appointments with fewer calls. Like water seeking its own level, a given number of cold calls eventually will produce a certain number of appointments.

When you start your apartment sales career, you should make as many cold calls as you can every day. Later, you can adjust your cold calling frequency according to the sales volume you can handle.

Whether you're just beginning your business or have been at it a long time, be sure to set aside specific times for cold calls and stick to your schedule without fail. When are the best times to phone prospects? Experience has proven that the most effective cold-call hours are between 9:30 and 11:30 in the morning, 1:30 and 4:30 in the afternoon and from 7:00 until 9:00 in the evening. Saturday and Sunday calls can make your weekends profitable, too.

Let's say you reserve the time between 1:30 and 3:30 in the afternoon every Monday, Wednesday and Friday for making phone contacts. Schedule your cold calling time on your calendar months in advance. Then, let nothing short of an earthquake interfere with those two hours twice a week. Ask your secretary to hold incoming calls for you, inform your co-workers that you have some important work to do, close your office door and get busy on the phone. Set your goals and keep your schedule. In almost no time, you'll feel relaxed and comfortable when you make your phone contacts and you'll be amazed at how rapidly your prospect list will grow. Your telephone will be your direct line to a bright, high-income future.

The time you spend cold calling can literally be the most valuable time of your life. Think of the rewards—thousands of dollars in commissions that can start with just a few minutes on the phone!

Meanwhile, let's put cold calling by phone on hold while we look at another way to help you start gathering prospects for apartment sales.

SUMMING UP WHAT YOU'VE LEARNED
IN CHAPTER 7

Your telephone is your direct line to potential apartment sales. Using your apartment catalog as a directory, keep these pointers in mind when you make your phone contacts.

1. The main purpose of your phone calls to apartment owners is to set up a personal meeting to discuss a sale.

2. Set a definite schedule for making cold calls and keep to that schedule without fail. The more cold calls you make, the better your chances for success.

3. Apartment owners are also apartment buyers. If the prospect isn't interested in selling, perhaps he or she may want to purchase another apartment property. Good questions during your phone conversations can turn up rewarding answers.

4. Be a good listener.

5. When you do make an appointment, try to schedule it in your office. You'll be on your own turf and you'll be able to show the client the large number of apartment properties in your catalog.

6. Note the date of your phone call to owners of apartment properties on the corresponding catalog sheet. Timing is important. Be sure to follow up with another call every six months.

7. Review the list of techniques for meeting prospects' objections, as described in this chapter.

8. Practice your phone skills by picking up the telephone and going through a dialog with an imaginary owner or buyer or role play with other agents in your office.

A Little Letter Can Go a Long Way

"Nothing great was ever achieved without enthusiasm."

—RALPH WALDO EMERSON

In the last chapter, we looked at ways of making cold calls to prospective apartment sellers and buyers—using the telephone to make the initial contact.

But what about the prospect who has an unlisted phone number? Or the busy investor whose secretary's main job is to ward off phone calls from unfamiliar names? Or the person who simply doesn't return phone calls? Here's where you call in the cavalry—the U.S. Postal Service—to help break through to the people you want to meet.

Despite the deluge of junk mail these days, nobody I know ever ignores a personally addressed letter with first-class postage on the envelope. And that's the way we're going to reach the prospects we cannot reach by phone. I say *we* because, as with every other sales technique in this book, I'm going to show you how to write contact letters that get results. However, keep in mind that prospect letters, no matter how expertly written, are no substitute for diligent cold calling. The best results are always achieved with as much personal contact as possible. You should use prospecting letters only when you are unable to reach an apartment owner by phone.

First, a few basics. I purposely used the phrase, "A Little Letter," in the title of this chapter to stress an important point: Keep your letter *brief*. You are asking for someone's reading time, and a long rambling letter could well end up as a paper airplane aimed at the wastebasket.

State the purpose of your letter in the first sentence. There's no need for a prolog. The faster you get to the point, the sooner your message will register with the recipient. A direct concise letter also portrays you as a clear thinker who knows how to make things move along.

Use compact sentences and short words. Don't try to impress anyone with your vocabulary. The sole purpose of your letter is to set up an appointment, not to deliver a dissertation on theoretical economics. Using long cumbersome sentences and complex words only puts rocks in your path.

Never send a handwritten letter to a sales prospect. All letters must be typewritten. You may have beautiful longhand writing skills, but the recipient will think (a) you are an amateur, not a serious professional, or (b) you can't afford a typewriter. And either of those impressions can be strikes against you.

If you are working in a professional real estate office, perhaps a full-time secretary will do your typing for you. Later in this chapter, I'll show you a simple method that will coordinate your letter-writing campaign with the typing pool. First, let's look at an example of the kind of sales contact letter that works. I know, because I've used this format successfully time and again. In this case, you're writing a letter to William Brookes, who owns an apartment building that fits the investment criteria of one of your prospective buyers. Mr. Brookes has an unlisted home phone number and none of the other sources listed in Chapter 6 will produce a business number; thus the following letter:

Dear Mr. Brookes:

I represent a client with a substantial amount of cash who is interested in purchasing 15 to 20 apartment units in the Hillcrest area. I have seen your Regents Court apartments at 1835 Willow Drive and they are the type of units for which my buyer would be interested in making an offer, given additional information concerning your property and the price and terms you would consider accepting.

If you are willing to entertain an offer on this property or any others that you own, please call me as soon as possible to discuss a potential sale.

Sincerely,

Look at the ground we've covered in this short letter that can be read in about 15 seconds. (Note that we take care to spell the apartment owner's name right. He is Mr. Brookes, not Brooks.)

1. The first sentence states the point of the letter. The reader instantly knows that your client is interested in buying a specific number of apartments in a definite area. As in making cold calls by phone, you allow some latitude by suggesting a range of units (15 to 20 in this case), instead of nailing down a single figure of, say 18 units, which can sound like too much of a coincidence, if that happens to be exactly the number of units in Mr. Brookes's building.

2. You refer to the property by name, instead of merely as "your apartment building." By doing so, you show the owner that you have seen the property and know its exact address.

3. You ask for additional information, including price and terms. Again, it pays to get straight to the point. Note, too, that you use the phrase, "interested in making an offer," instead of stating that your client *will* make an offer. You are seeking information for a *potential* buyer and you must be careful to avoid making commitments or misleading statements.

4. In the second paragraph you use that important word, *entertain* (an offer) to suggest that the owner thoughtfully consider a sale. No pressure, no obligation.

5. You also inquire about "any others [apartments] that you own." Mr. Brookes may not want to sell his Regents Court property, but he could very well want to dispose of another apartment building. And that fact will present you with additional sales opportunities.

A couple of other observations. This letter, like all effective sales messages, uses active verbs—action words—rather than passive ones. For example, directly saying, "I represent a client who is interested...," carries much more power than an oblique statement such as, "A possible purchase offer could be made by a client represented by me." Again, "...please call me as soon as possible..." is far stronger than "A phone call at your convenience would be appreciated." Why be timid? To paraphrase an old saying, "Faint heart never won a sale."

The most effective way to approach your letter-writing campaign is as follows. Type a copy of the letter we just reviewed, inserting blanks for the pertinent information. Here's an example:

_____

Owner's name

_____

_____

Owner's address

                                            _____

                                            Date

Dear _____ :
    I represent a client with a substantial amount of cash who is interested in purchasing _____ to _____ units in the _____ area. I have seen your _____ _____ apartments at _____ _____ and they are the type of units for which my client would be interested in making an offer, given additional information concerning your property and the price and terms you would consider accepting.
    If you are willing to entertain an offer on this property or any others that you own, please call me as soon as possible to discuss a potential sale.

Sincerely,

Next, make 25 to 50 photocopies of the letter. As you move through the pages of your property catalog while cold calling, you will come across the buildings whose owners' phone numbers you cannot locate. In those cases, simply fill in the blanks on the contact letter. When you're through cold calling, give the accumulated completed letters (to the owners who had no listed phone numbers) to your secretary to be individually typed.

    If you're fortunate enough to have a word processor in your office, you can keep the blank letter on a magnetic disk. Your secretary can transfer the appropriate information into the machine and the final results can be printed and mailed in a short period of time. Always include your business card. (If you use a word processor, be sure you have a letter quality printer. Anything looking like a computerized form letter will find its way quickly to the trash can.)

Since you could be sending several contact letters at once, you may be wondering how to keep the various buildings separate in your mind when you get a response. Easy. When Mr. Brookes calls to say he's received your letter and has an interest in selling, simply say, "Yes Mr. Brookes, what is the building's property address?" When he's told you, reach for your catalog binder and look up the building. Since your catalog sheets are organized alphabetically by street name, you'll quickly be able to find the sheet with the picture of the building attached. You can then respond with a remark like, "Yes, Mr. Brookes, those are the Regent Court apartments, the building with the beautiful landscaping," or something similar. You can then move right into the same approach as if you had reached Mr. Brookes with a cold call to get an appointment to meet him by getting additional information concerning the property.

Even those contact letters that do not immediately produce an appointment with an apartment owner are worthwhile. Let's say you hear from a Mrs. Johnson, to whom you had written an inquiry letter about her apartment building. She phones you to say she is not interested in selling her property. At least you've made it to first base by getting her to respond to your letter. And this brings us to another kind of important correspondence—a follow-up letter to those property owners with whom you have made a phone contact. Your letter should say something like this:

Dear Mrs. Johnson:

Thank you for allowing me the opportunity to introduce myself on the phone last Tuesday. I am a commercial real estate agent specializing in the sale of apartment properties.

Although you indicated that you are not interested in selling your Western Horizons apartments on Mercedes Drive at this time, I'm enclosing my card as a reference for your future real estate needs.

Sincerely,

EVERYONE SELLS SOMETIME

Let's backtrack briefly. Remember, the whole purpose of this book is to help you build a profitable enjoyable future for yourself by selling apartment properties. All the letters you write and the phone calls you make to apartment owners are part of the ongoing process of enhancing your career.

Every contact you make can be like money in the bank. Why? Because sooner or later, every apartment owner sells his or her property—usually within about five years of the date of purchase, as mentioned in Chapter 4. When that time comes, you want your name to be uppermost in the mind of the building owner.

Speaking from my personal experience, I can assure you that writing introductory and follow-up letters—*always* with your business card attached—pays dividends. In a number of cases, apartment owners have called me as long as *two years* after my first contact with them. They kept my card and therefore kept me in mind when they decided to place their building on the market.

TELL WHAT YOU SELL

Once you begin to sell, tell the world about it! People like to deal with achievers, and you owe it to yourself to let apartment owners and buyers know that you are the person to put a deal together. So don't be bashful. Again, here's where the right kind of letter comes in.

When escrow has closed on one of your apartment transactions, turn to your catalog and select the names of owners whose buildings are in the same general area in which you made your sale. Then, write a letter such as the following:

Dear _____:

I recently sold the Valley Vista Apartments at 4806 Palo Verde Way for $1,200,000. Because this property is in the same neighborhood as your apartment building on Canyon Court, I thought you might be interested in learning of the transaction.

If you are considering selling the Green Briar Villas, I would like to meet with you to provide a detailed market analysis of your property. This comprehensive evaluation will include a rental survey, recent comparable sales figures and a probable sales price for your property. Since you have owned the Green Briar Villas for over five years, you may also want to look at the advantages that a tax-deferred exchange could bring.

I'll be pleased to meet with you at your convenience. Just give me a call at 555-0000.

Sincerely,

No bragging, no boasting. Just an informative helpful letter to an apartment owner who could be your next client. As you make more sales, you'll want to say so by adding a sentence (with appropriate figures) that says, for example, "In the past 18 months, I have sold 180 apartment units, with a total value of over $7 million dollars." To emphasize a basic point of this book, you must steadily build awareness of your stature and growth in the apartment-selling business.

LOG YOUR LETTERS

Whenever you send out any letter—an inquiry, a thank-you or a report on the sales you've made—be sure to note the mailing date on the catalog sheet that describes the recipient's property. From time to time, scan the catalog pages and make follow-up contacts in the future. The same goes for phone calls you make to apartment owners. Note the dates and keep in touch.

TIPS ON EFFECTIVE LETTERS

Direct-mail specialists, particularly the large national firms that spend millions of dollars a year on mail advertising campaigns, have sales letter writing down to a science. They know what works and what doesn't. At no extra charge, I'm passing along these principles that cost major companies a fortune to discover by trial and error over the years.

You may be surprised to learn the three elements noted by a direct mail recipient *before* he or she reads the letter itself. First, most people read the *inside address.* If the letter greets them with "Dear Friend," "Dear Car Owner," or such, the letter stands only a limited chance of being read further. If recipients see the letter addressed to them by name, they next read the *signature* on the letter. If readers note that the letter is signed by a person with an executive title or someone with authority in making transactions (in your case, a sales agent or broker), they tend to accept the letter's credibility. (*Tip:* Give yourself a title or at least a special designation. After your name, add a phrase like "Apartment Sales Consultant," "Commercial Real Estate Agent," "Apartment Marketing Specialist" or other term that describes your area of activity. There is nothing tricky or dishonest about assigning a title to yourself. You *are* a specialist and consultant in apartment marketing. Say so under your signature.)

What do you think is the next element the direct-mail recipient reads? The letter itself? Guess again. It's the *postscript.* You may think of a postscript as an afterthought, a little tidbit without much value. However, direct-mail marketers know that a postscript is a strong element in a sales letter. Keep this fact in mind whenever you contact a prospect by mail. Your letter definitely will gain more attention with an intriguing postscript. Try it and prove it to yourself. The following are sample postscripts for various kinds of letters. (Obviously, each postscript must apply to a specific message and must be true.)

> P.S. My client is leaving on an extended trip on Tuesday, June 8. I suggest we get together before that date if you're interested in discussing a sale.

> P.S. Since you have owned the Concord Heights apartments for almost five years, you may want to consider trading your property for one that could deliver better tax benefits.

> P.S. I have one of the most extensive catalog files of apartment properties in this entire area. I'd be pleased to show you a wide selection of apartment buildings in a short visit to my office at your convenience.

Anyway, you get the idea. If you want to highlight a special aspect of your business, or want to insert a note of urgency in your letter, add a postscript to suit the situation.

THE IMPORTANCE OF TIMING

Good salespeople know the value of proper timing in reaching prospects. To make sure that your prospecting letters arrive at the most advantageous time, here are some tested guidelines:

1. You know, of course, that mailing a business letter during the Christmas season can be a waste of time and postage. People are more interested in holiday cheer than in business at that time. In fact, because most individuals need a week or so to prepare for and then recover from the jolly season, it's a good idea to avoid mailing prospect letters during the entire period from December 15 to January 10.

2. Studies of direct mail effectiveness show that the most productive months for mailings are January (after the 10th), February, August and October. June is historically the worst mailing month of all. The month probably ranks at the bottom because it's when most people start thinking of summer vacation; they tend to put off business decisions until later.

3. Direct mail experts have also found that sales letters should not arrive during the first five or six days of any month. People tend to busy themselves with trying to catch up on all the things they failed to complete the month before and are not in the most receptive state of mind. The arrival of most bills around the first of the month doesn't create a happy mood either.

4. Tuesday, Wednesday and Thursday during the last three weeks of the month are the most opportune times for your sales letters to arrive. Avoid mailing letters to reach the recipient on a Monday or Friday. Many individuals are depressed on Mondays, the back-to-the-grind days, and may also be swamped with a pile of mail that landed during the weekend. On Fridays, most people are winding things down for the weekend ahead. Friday also tends to be a put-off day for many business executives. They often keep the incoming mail out of sight and out of mind while they reserve tee times for the weekend.

The preceding guidelines are not chiseled in granite and, like all rules, they certainly allow room for exceptions. However, they do represent longtime experience by successful direct-mail marketers and for that reason they're worth knowing.

GETTING YOUR MESSAGE TO THE MEDIA

While this chapter primarily concerns the use of letters in contacting prospects, I do want to note another means of bringing your progress to the attention of your prospects: the business section of local and regional newspapers, both daily and weekly publications.

When you make an apartment sale, write a brief press release and mail it—or better yet, hand deliver it—to the business editor of your area's newspapers. You'll find most editors quite receptive to your news story, especially if it is brief and totally factual.

After all, editors depend on a steady supply of news items to create their sections of the paper.

How do you write a press release? Easily. Just use the old who, what, where and when news formula, like this:

SUNRISE HEIGHTS APARTMENTS SOLD FOR $800,000

The 20-unit Sunrise Heights Apartments at 5235 Golden Trail, General City, were sold last week for $800,000 to Elizabeth A. Burnett. The building contains 7 two-bedroom/one-bath units and 13 one-bedroom/one-bath units.

First National Savings and Loan made the first trust deed loan of $600,000, and the seller, Charles C. Swanson, carried back a second trust deed in the amount of $40,000.

Betty Martin, apartment marketing specialist for ABC Realty, Inc., represented both parties in the transaction.

And thus you have your press release. You don't have to be a trained journalist. Just put down the facts and let the editor take it from there. To get the hang of writing news releases, read the ones you see in your newspaper and copy their basic structure. News release formats are generic, so there is no plagiarism involved.

Publicize your sales closings at every opportunity. Doing so is one the most productive ways to spread your reputation as a successful apartment salesperson. (*Tip.* Make photocopies of your news releases when they appear in the newspaper and include them with your letters to prospects.)

Now, you're ready to meet with apartment sellers and buyers. I'll show you how to put the players together in the next chapter.

SUMMING UP WHAT YOU'VE LEARNED
IN CHAPTER 8

Writing prospect letters to apartment owners who cannot be reached by phone can effectively set the stage for a personal appointment. Review the following key points as guidelines for your letter-writing campaign.

1. Keep your letters short and state your purpose in the first sentence.

2. All letters should be typed, never handwritten.

3. Mention the name and address of the owner's apartment building—not merely "your apartment property."

4. Give yourself a title, such as "Apartment Sales Consultant," "Apartment Marketing Specialist" or other designation that describes your role and gives you a position of authority.

5. Turn out more prospect letters in less time by copying the fill-in-the-blanks format shown on page 108.

6. As you make sales, be sure to mention the most recent ones in your prospect letters. People like to deal with winners.

7. Time your mailings so that your letters do not arrive too close to a holiday, on a Friday or Monday or during the first five or six days of the month.

8. Note the date of each letter on the page of your catalog that describes the owner's property.

9. Scan your catalog to remind yourself of letters previously mailed to apartment owners. Follow up with further contact letters.

CHAPTER 9

Meeting the Seller

*"It is better to know some of the
questions than all of the answers."*

—JAMES THURBER

Here's where it all begins to come together.

Everything you've learned up to this point—gaining market knowledge, pricing apartments, building a catalog, making cold calls—all of this has a single purpose: to help you put together an apartment sale and earn your first commission!

This means you are now ready to meet the seller with whom you've made an appointment by phone.

You can genuinely look forward to this first visit with a seller because you have a great deal going for you. By using the methods in this book, you know your marketplace inside and out. You know the prevailing rents. You know the sales prices of comparable buildings. You also know the various appraisal techniques to enable you to easily determine the value of any apartment building. And, of course, if you need to refresh your memory on any point before your meeting with the seller, just check back to the chapter on that subject. You'll find this book a ready reference guide at every stage of your career.

You have at your disposal the knowledge you require. All you need now is experience and that will come more quickly than you may think. In fact, you can be so confident of your ability that your sales prospect won't even know he or she is your first client. That's why it is so important to be guided by two words: *Be prepared.* You've worked hard to get that appointment and if you handle things right, you could virtually walk away with a sale.

Before you ever meet your prospective seller in person, aim for a sale by mentally steering straight toward the single, all-important factor of *seller motivation.*

In selling apartments, as in all commercial transactions, motivation is the fuel that powers the sales engine. It is the *reason* for an apartment owner to consider selling his or her property. Here you play detective to discover that motivation.

Knowing what can motivate an apartment owner to sell his or her property is vital for three sound reasons. This knowledge can (1) keep the seller's attention focused on the main reason for selling, (2) guide you in verbally supporting his or her reason to sell the building and (3) help you structure the sale to suit the seller's needs.

DISCOVERING SELLER MOTIVATIONS

Before your meeting with the seller, review the various situations that can persuade an apartment owner to put property on the market. Knowing these possible reasons can lead you to ask the right questions during your meeting.

Look for Personal Motives. Maybe a couple of bad resident managers have driven the owner up the wall, driving him or her to leave personnel headaches behind. Perhaps there's been a divorce or death in the family. Or the owner could have a chronic illness that makes it difficult for him or her to remain involved in apartment operations. Perhaps he or she and his or her partner aren't on speaking terms and he or she wants to get away from an unpleasant alliance. Maybe the owner wants to move to another state to be closer to his or her grandchildren. Personal situations can be powerful factors in business decisions. Look for them. When an owner doesn't directly state his or her reasons for selling, use your intuition as an antenna to pick up signals. Good hunches pay.

What's Happening in the Marketplace? This is an important question to keep in mind during your meeting with a potential seller. If the apartment market in your area is especially hot, now could be an ideal time for the owner to cash in on a high price. On the other hand, negative market factors such as a rise in the vacancy rate could also prompt the owner to dispose of his or her property. Perhaps the motivation has to do with alterations in the character of the neighborhood. Here is where your market knowledge can serve you well in suggesting and reinforcing reasons for the owner to consider selling.

Consider Investment Values. Be ready to explore the possibility of a profit for the owner. He may not be aware of how much his property has increased in value since he bought it. Or perhaps the owner needs to liquidate the property to meet a large note that is coming due. The property might need a lot of costly repairs; selling would be a smart way to escape those big expenses. Then too, the owner's tax benefits might be declining and a sale at this time could be an intelligent move. A negative cash flow may have become too much of a burden. These are all factors that could trigger a sale.

If you're lucky, you may have discovered the owner's sales motivation when you contacted him by phone. In that case, you can reinforce his reason for selling when you meet him in person. If you don't know his reason for considering a sale (maybe he isn't totally sure), understanding basic seller motivations can help you find the right verbal buttons to push.

IMPORTANT FIRST STEPS

To make sure you're as well prepared as you can be, here are other important steps to take before your meeting with a seller.

Step 1. Drive by the property and review it once again to update your judgment of the building and the neighborhood. Property conditions can change rapidly and you'll want to know the exact status of the building when you meet with the owner. This drive-by is especially significant after you've been in the business for a while and have accumulated a large amount of apartment information in your catalog. The appearance of the apartment complex may have changed considerably since you first took a picture of it.

Obvious changes in property conditions can also give you a clue to factors motivating the owner to sell. Deteriorating maintenance, for example, can reflect serious problems with management or cash flow. "For Rent" signs may indicate an increase in vacancies, or you might spot a meaningful change in the character of the neighborhood that could affect property values.

Step 2. If possible, research ownership records for any other properties owned by the seller (see Chapter 6). This investigation will not only give you additional background information on your prospect, but may also help you uncover potential sales motivations. The seller, for instance, may own other apartment buildings in scattered locations and may want to consolidate management responsibilities by disposing of one or more properties in the outer areas of your territory. Or this individual may own a number of office buildings and may want to sell his or her one or two apartment properties so that he can concentrate on his or her leased commercial investments.

Step 3. Prepare a rental survey and research comparable sales data and on-the-market comparables for the area in which the owner's property is located. Having this information in hand when you meet with the seller has valuable advantages. First, it establishes your credibility for appraising the property. Second, it provides you with facts and figures to guide the owner to a realistic view of the value of the property. Consequently, you'll have the supporting data you need to help answer the seller's questions and meet possible objections relating to your market judgment of his or her apartment building.

Step 4. Review any notes you made during your cold call to the apartment owner. As stated earlier, you may have discovered his or her sales motivation or other pertinent data that will aid you during your person-to-person meeting.

MEETING THE OWNER

You've arrived for your appointment (on time) and you've introduced yourself in person to the apartment owner you have contacted by phone.

You instantly begin to establish your credibility by reminding the owner that you are a specialist in the apartment sales field and are very active in the marketplace. Express a sincere interest in his or her property and let him or her know that you are well acquainted with his neighborhood. In later meetings with other owners, you'll want to further establish your credentials by telling the seller the dollar amount of apartment properties you've sold in the past year. And if you've handled the sales of another building near his or her, you'll certainly want to mention that transaction.

Next, make sure you are dealing with an authorized decision maker. If the person with whom you are talking is the sole owner of the apartment building, you're on solid ground. In the event the owner holds title jointly with a spouse, ask if the spouse needs to be involved in the decision to sell the property. If so, request that he or she join the meeting. In cases where the owner is actually a partnership or syndicate, determine whether your prospect has the legal authority to speak for the coowners. If not, suggest another meeting at a later date with all the decision makers present. At the start of your career, you might be tempted to go ahead with a meeting with only one member of a partnership, especially if he assures you that he will personally present your recommendations to the partners. Usually that pass-along information gets distorted somewhere along the way and you'll need to set up a group meeting just to straighten things out.

Assuming you have all the necessary parties present, go on to establish the credibility of your *buyer*. Doing so is extremely important because the seller will want to know at the outset that a potential buyer exists and that he or she has the financial ability to close the transaction. Inform the owner that your buyer is a local investor, that he or she owns other apartment properties (if those facts are the case), that he or she is financially qualified, and that his or her capital is readily available. You'll also want to add any other relevant facts that demonstrate your buyer's ability to perform if the two parties can come to terms regarding the sale of the property.

Reminder: If you don't already know the key motivating factor that will prompt an owner to sell an apartment building, keep probing for that information. Here again is where it pays to be a good listener. Pick up whatever clues you can. Maybe the owner will make a comment about being tired of apartment management. Or he may mention that he's taking a close look at his tax situation. Retirement might be just ahead for him. Be ready to bolster any reason he may have to sell his apartment building. And don't be afraid to ask direct questions about his plans for the future. Aren't *you* pleased when someone shows an interest in your ideas about the years ahead?

At this point, let me insert a note of helpful realism. If, no matter how diligently you seek a motive for selling, you find that the owner has no desire whatsoever to market his property, it's best to cordially end the conversation and move on to more productive possibilities. Even though, in your initial cold call, the owner may have stated that he was interested in entertaining an offer to sell his property, he may merely be looking for a free property appraisal. Occasionally this happens, but you can use such an experience as a sales lesson. Every time you meet with a prospective client, you will improve your selling skills. And as I've said before, since most buildings sell at some point, you may have laid the groundwork for a sale at a later date. You must keep moving along because you cannot *create* more time as you need it; you can only *manage* your time. Therefore, work only with motivated owners whose buildings have a high probability of being sold. The sooner you say good-bye to time wasters, the sooner you will succeed in your career.

Having noted the need to deal only with serious prospects, let's continue your first meeting with an apartment owner.

By now, you've established a good rapport with the owner. He knows you understand your business and are eager to help him advance his interests.

You can move things along as follows: "Mr. Green, as I told you on the phone, if my buyer is to make an intelligent decision concerning the purchase of your property, I'm going to need some additional information about the building."

Having said that, it's important for you to explain the appraisal process to make the owner feel comfortable about answering your questions. Remember, even though you've made a good impression on him, he still doesn't know you. Therefore, he may be reluctant to give you detailed financial information without knowing why you need such data.

Welcome the opportunity to fully explain property evaluation methods. First, this opportunity gives you another way of underscoring your credibility and professionalism. Second, you can now prepare your prospect to accept a realistic market value of his property. And third, you'll quickly discover the owner's level of sophistication when you begin talking about determining market values according to the gross rent multiplier method, the capitalization approach, price per unit and price per square foot. (To refresh your memory about the ways to determine market values, review Chapter 3.) Sensing how much your prospect knows about market values helps you adjust your end of the conversation accordingly. Talking at your prospect's comfort level helps maintain friendly rapport.

Once you have thoroughly explained how you arrive at market values, take out a property data sheet and an income and expense summary (as shown in Figures 9–1 and 9–2) and start filling in the answers to key questions about the property.

The property data sheet (Figure 9–1) is similar, with a few notable exceptions, to the rental survey form we discussed in Chapter 2. Categories have been added for the gross and net rentable square footages of the property. Recording this information will enable you to compute the building's price per square foot. In addition, room has been allowed to note the condition of the apartment interiors and the age of the roof. In Chapter 3 we discussed the need to make an allowance in price for any substantial costs associated with bringing rental rates to market levels. In your interview with the owner you can query him about the condition of the unit interiors, including carpets, drapes, paint and appliances. Also, a deteriorating roof or aging water heaters can be costly items to replace and you'll want to know their condition. Under *existing financing*, include the present loans against the property. There could be some favorable financing that the buyer may want to assume.

The "Income and Expense Summary" (Figure 9–2) is self-explanatory and should be filled out as completely as possible. One of the best ways to obtain accurate expense information is to have the owner show you the previous year's tax return concerning the property.

When I meet with an owner for the first time, I always show him exactly how I arrive at the market value of his property. Walking the owner step-by-step through the appraisal process demonstrates the logic of what you are saying and proves that you work in a thoroughly professional way.

(*Note*: It's very important that you do this appraisal right then and there, during your first meeting with the owner. Having to go back to your office to do your computations and then trying to contact the owner at a later date could cost you a sale. Allowing the owner too much time to think things over (and possibly discuss the sale with relatives and neighbors) often results in

FIGURE 9-1   Property Data Sheet

No. of Units _____ No. of Buildings _____ No. of Stories _____

Age _____ Age of Roof _____ Lot Size _____ Alley _____

Building Area: Gross Sq. Ft.* _____ Net Rentable Sq. Ft.* _____

Parking Spaces (covered) _____ / (uncovered) _____ / (garages) _____

Disposals_____ Dishwashers_____ Refrigerators_____ Ranges_____

Carpets _____ Drapes _____ Pool _____ Rec. Room _____ Sauna _____

Patios/Balconies_____ Air Cond._____ Utilities_____

Other Features _____

Interior Condition _____

_____

*Measurements are approximate.

Existing Financing

Loan	Amount	Lender	Int. Rate	Due	Payment	Assumable
1st	_____	_____	_____	_____	_____	_____
2nd	_____	_____	_____	_____	_____	_____
3rd	_____	_____	_____	_____	_____	_____

Unit Mix and Rent Schedule

Number	Br/Ba.	Sq. Ft.	Current Rent	Market Rent
_____	___	_____	$ _____	$ _____
_____	___	_____	_____	_____
_____	___	_____	_____	_____
Monthly Laundry Income			_____	_____
Monthly Gross Income			_____	_____
Annual Gross Income			$ _____	$ _____

FIGURE 9–2 Income and Expense Summary

	Actual	Projected
Scheduled gross income	$ _____	$ _____
less vacancy allowance (%)	_____	_____
Effective gross income	$ _____	$ _____
Expenses:		
Management (professional)	$ _____	$ _____
Management (on-site resident manager)	_____	_____
Property taxes	_____	_____
Insurance	_____	_____
Water	_____	_____
Gas & electricity	_____	_____
Maintenance and repairs	_____	_____
Pool service	_____	_____
Pest control service	_____	_____
Trash removal	_____	_____
Gardener	_____	_____
Supplies	_____	_____
Other	_____	_____
Less total expenses	$ _____	$ _____
Net operating income	$ _____	$ _____

"seller's remorse," a malady as bad as the dreaded "buyer's remorse." Furthermore, calculating a feasible market price right on the spot demonstrates both your capability and your efficiency in getting things done.)

Your facts and figures are now on paper. Using my own approach as a guide, you can say, "Mr. Green, based on the condition and location of your property, the overall picture of what you have to offer, and what comparable apartments are selling for in this area, I feel that the fair market value of your building is $400,000 (or whatever your appraisal indicates) and that is the price that I feel my buyer would most likely be willing to pay for the property." You should then also suggest to the seller that the property be presented to the buyer at a slightly higher price, perhaps $415,000, to give the seller some bargaining room in which to negotiate. Strong practical and psychological reasons exist for handling pricing this way. (We'll discuss those reasons in more detail in Chapters 10 and 11.)

To back up your appraisal, you'll also want to show the owner the sale prices of recently sold comparable buildings.

As we noted in the beginning of this chapter, having comparable sales data is very important. You'll have the supporting information you need to verify your appraisal value. This information is especially useful when you're dealing with an owner who thinks his building is worth more than your appraisal indicates. In such cases, you can make a persuasive point by showing him a comparable building that has been for sale for a long time but has not sold because it is overpriced. This type of comparison is called an on-the-market comparable. With your comparable sales data, you can clearly demonstrate that the owner's price expectations are unrealistic. The owner will have a hard time arguing with you because the facts will speak for themselves.

Assuming that the owner is interested in pursuing a sale at the recommended price, the next move is to determine the terms. Does the owner need an all-cash sale? Is he or she willing to carry back part of the financing? How much down payment will be needed? What kind of purchase arrangement will best suit his or her tax situation?

The final step in this stage of the transaction is to qualify the seller. You read it right—the *seller*. After reviewing your appraisal process, ask directly, "If my buyer will make an offer for your property with the price and terms we've just discussed, will you sell your building at this time?"

You may as well know immediately whether you have a viable sales possibility. If the owner is undecided, try to determine the reason for his or her hesitation and attempt to set a date for a decision.

Finally, a word about listings. Are they necessary in selling apartments? Speaking from experience, I can say that a listing is somewhat like an umbrella. You don't absolutely need one, but it's nice to have in case of rain.

Several important reasons exist for having a listing, even one of short duration. First, the listing spells out in writing the price and terms that the owner has agreed to accept. Second, it specifies and protects your commission in the event you or another broker sells the property during the term of the listing. Third, the listing affords you greater control over the situation in that you will have a broader degree of latitude to steer the transaction in the direction you want. You may not be able to successfully negotiate a deal with the buyer you originally had in mind. A listing maintains your connection with the owner so that you can further market the property to other clients and brokers. Fourth, a listing gives you additional credibility with a *buyer*—your present one or someone else. Being able to say, "I have a listing on the Rosewood Garden Apartments" assures your buyer that he will not be merely on a fishing expedition if he makes an offer to purchase the property. Last, but very important, a listing cements in writing the owner's decision to sell and affirms that you are dealing with a genuine business matter and not playing a frivolous game.

You can approach the subject of obtaining the listing by explaining to the owner that your buyer will want to know that he is working with a serious seller and that he is not wasting his time in pursuing the purchase of the building. A signed listing agreement stating the asking price and terms will convince the buyer of the owner's motivation to sell and eliminate any confusion about what the owner wants for the property. Try to obtain a 60- to 90-day listing by explaining to the owner that in case a deal cannot be made with the buyer you currently represent, you can continue to present the property to other buyers you have as well as other apartment brokers. Because you are familiar with the owner and his or her property, you can be his best representative.

In cases where the owner is reluctant to give you a two- or three-month listing, ask for a listing of just a week or two. A *week* or two? Yes, because building owners normally will not object to such a short listing and, if you have qualified the buyer properly and priced the property correctly, you should be able to negotiate the sale between the parties in that amount of time. If, however, at the end of that brief period, you have not been able to consummate a purchase agreement, you can then very likely extend the listing for a longer term. By now, the owner has invested his or her time in the sale of the property and probably has made an even firmer commitment to dispose of the building. He or she is personally involved in dealing with you and, if you have been professional and diligent in your work, he or she should be pleased with the job you have already done. Therefore, he or she is more likely to go along with you instead of starting all over again with another broker. In other words, you have your foot in the door. Keep it there.

Remember, as I said before, a listing is nice but it is not always necessary. Your most important goal is to make the sale! There are some owners who just will not give a listing but are motivated to sell when presented with the right offer. If you can't obtain a listing but have concluded that the owner is motivated to sell the property, continue your efforts by breaking a speed record in getting the information to your buyer for his evaluation. To modify an old saying, action speaks louder than listings.

One other word of advice: In every conversation with an apartment owner, keep your eye steadily on your one and only goal— to *make a sale*. Chatting about the owner's kids and dog is okay for openers, but always guide the talk back to your single purpose. Your future is tremendously important, and the more you are able to control the seller-buyer situation, the greater the amount of income you will earn. And your clients will truly appreciate your dedication to your career and your confident skilled way of conducting business. People like doers, so go ahead and do it!

Next, let's look at how to handle purchase offers. That's where the money is.

SUMMING UP WHAT YOU'VE LEARNED
IN CHAPTER 9

After making an appointment with a seller by phone, you can make your meeting productive by using the methods described in this chapter. As a reminder, here are some of the most important guidelines.

1. *Be prepared.* Drive by the property before your meeting. Update your judgment of the building and the neighborhood. Be aware of any changes since you first saw the property.

2. Bring your rental survey and comparable sales data on other apartment properties in the area.

3. Review any notes you may have made during your cold call to the owner.

4. Arrive at the meeting on time!

5. Try to discover the owner's *motivation*, the central reason to consider putting the property on the market.

6. Let the owner know that you have a qualified buyer who is ready to make an offer if the price and terms are right.

7. Fill out a complete property data sheet using the format shown in this chapter.

8. Fully explain your property evaluation methods to back your suggested market price.

9. Try to get a listing—even one for only a week or two.

CHAPTER 10

Making the Offer

*"With regard to excellence, it is
not enough to know, but we must
try to have and use it."*

—ARISTOTLE

Now, as Sherlock Holmes would put it, the plot thickens as we get ready to bring your buyer on stage. But let's leave him waiting in the wings for a few moments while we determine exactly how we will go about creating a purchase offer for an apartment property.

In the preceding chapter, you learned how to get an owner into the act by meeting with him or her, discovering motivations to sell, filling out a property information sheet and obtaining a listing.

So far, so good. Next, we are going to work with the buyer in a three-part process:

1. putting together the property information for the buyer
2. structuring the offer
3. presenting the offer to the seller

With the above points on our road map, let's follow the route to a successful sale. Study each step carefully and don't try to take any shortcuts because, as with all instructions in this book, the techniques you are about to learn are my tried and proven methods of successfully selling apartments. Every step has a definite purpose.

PUTTING TOGETHER PROPERTY INFORMATION

After meeting with an apartment owner who is interested in selling, you have collected considerable information about the property. The first step is to put this data into presentable form. Remember, you are a *professional* and that image will suffer if you simply hand a prospective buyer a few sheets of scribbled notes and figures. Buying an apartment building is a major transaction and the information you present to the buyer must be complete and of the greatest clarity to enable your client to make an intelligent investment decision about the property.

First, prepare a *pro forma*, or property description. This *pro forma* ("provided in advance") is actually a detailed profile—physical and financial—of the apartment property you want your buyer to consider. The information in the *pro forma* really serves two purposes: to give your prospective buyer a quick and comprehensive view of the apartment property and to describe the property to other brokers in the event your buyer decides not to purchase the building. Either way, you'll want your work to reflect your stature as a top-caliber apartment specialist.

Study the sample *pro forma* on the following pages. I'll explain various items as we go along.

First, the cover page (Figure 10–1).

The cover page instantly tells the buyer (or another broker) the name of the property, the number of units, the location and your status as the listing agent. The faster you get to the point, the better. If you were not able to obtain an exclusive listing, simply leave out the word *exclusively* and state instead *offered by* in front of your name.

Please note, too, the disclaimer at the bottom of the cover page: "The information contained in this *pro forma* has been obtained from reliable sources and is believed to be accurate, but it is not guaranteed to be correct." Always add this critically important statement for your own protection. It means exactly what it says—that although you secured information on the property from the owner, you personally cannot ensure the accuracy of the data. Sometimes mistakes happen. The property manager may have kept poor records or an owner may inadvertently have given you incorrect information. In any event, that disclaimer is valuable protection for you.

FIGURE 10–1 *Pro Forma*

**PLAZA DEL SOL APARTMENTS
28 UNITS**

(Picture of the property)

425 Sage Brush Lane
Phoenix, Arizona
Exclusively offered by Mary Price

The information contained in this *pro forma* has been obtained from reliable sources and is believed to be accurate, but it is not guaranteed to be correct.

FIGURE 10–2   Price, Down Payment and Proposed Financing

Price $ 1,350,000

Down payment   350,000

Proposed financing:

   1st Mortgage $ 800,000

      New conventional loan at 10% interest, 30 year amortization.
      Monthly payment of $7,021.

   2d Mortgage $ 200,000

      Owner carry back at 9.75% interest only monthly payments,
      with the entire balance all due 7 years from close of escrow.
      Monthly payment of $1,625.

Financial Analysis

Gross rent multiplier: Actual ___8.48___ / Projected ___7.81___

Capitalization rate: Actual ___7.78___ / Projected ___8.19___

                 Price per unit: __48,214__   Price per sq. ft. __$49.09__

FIGURE 10-3 Property Data Sheet

Property Data Sheet

No. of Units __28__ No. of Buildings __3__ No. of Stories __2__

Age __10__ Age of Roof __New__ Lot Size __100 × 224__ Alley __yes__

Building Area: Gross Sq. Ft.* __27,500__ Net Rentable Sq. Ft.* __24,200__

Parking Spaces (covered) __20__ / (uncovered) __22__ / (garages) __0__

Disposals __28__ Dishwashers __21__ Refrigerators __28__ Ranges __28__

Carpets __28__ Drapes __28__ Pool __yes__ Rec. Rm. __yes__ Sauna __no__

Patios/Balconies __yes__ Air Cond. __yes__ Utilities __tenants pay G+E__

Other Features __Two-bedroom units have outside storage closets.__

Interior Condition __16 of the units have had new carpet in the last two years.__

Other items are reported in good to excellent condition.

*Measurements are approximate.

Existing Financing

Loan	Amount	Lender	Int. Rate	Due	Payment	Assumable
1st	$420,000	City Federal	9.75%	2008	$3,608	no
2nd	$ 35,000	Private	10%	1990	$ 292	no
3rd	N/A					

Unit Mix and Rent Schedule

Number	Br/Ba	Sq. Ft.	Current Rent	Market Rent
7	1/1	675	$ 375–385	$ 415
16	2/2	880	460–485	525
5	3/2	1080	565	595
Monthly Laundry Income			130	130
Monthly Gross Income			13,270	14,410
Annual Gross Income			$ 159,240	$ 172,920

FIGURE 10-4   Income and Expense Summary

Income and Expense Summary		
	Actual	*Projected*
Scheduled gross income	$ 159,240	$ 172,920
less vacancy allowance (5%)	− 7,962	− 8,646
Effective gross income	$ 151,278	$ 164,274
Expenses:		
Management (professional)	$ N/A	$ N/A
Management (on-site resident manager)	8,200	8,200
Property taxes	9,500	14,000
Insurance	1,700	2,300
Water	5,520	5,520
Gas & electricity	7,260	7,260
Maintenance and repairs	7,140	9,500
Pool service	1,200	1,200
Pest control service	350	350
Trash removal	1,044	1,044
Gardener	3,158	3,158
Supplies	1,120	1,120
Other	0	0
Less total expenses	$ − 46,192	$ − 53,652
Net operating income	$ 105,086	$ 110,622

FIGURE 10-5   Investment Analysis (Three-Year Projection)

INVESTMENT ANALYSIS (Three-Year Projection)

	Year 1	Year 2*	Year 3*
Projected annual income	$ 172,920	$ 181,566	$ 190,644
less vacancy (5%)	− 8,646	− 9,078	− 9,532
Effective income	164,274	172,488	181,112
less projected annual expenses	− 53,652	− 56,334	− 59,150
Net operating income	110,622	116,154	121,962
less debt service	−103,752	−103,752	−103,752
Cash flow	6,870	12,402	18,210
less depreciation**	− 34,364	− 34,364	− 34,364
Taxable income (or loss)	$ <27,494>	$ <21,962>	$ <16,154>
Valuation at 7.8 × Projected Income	$ 1,350,000	$ 1,416,000	$ 1,487,000

*Assumes a 5% increase in annual income and expenses.

**Straight line method using 27.5 recovery period and 70% improvement value.

Additional Comments:___The Plaza Del Sol is a pride-of-ownership apartment___
complex located in a prime rental area of Phoenix. The property is attractively
laid out and landscaped with all units featuring spacious interiors and modern
amenities.

The second page of the *pro forma* (Figure 10–2) contains the seller's asking price and proposed financing terms and a brief financial analysis of the transaction. Be sure to show the gross rent multiplier and cap rate using *projected* as well as *actual* rents. This way, the buyer has a truer perspective of the situation and you have a better shot at convincing the buyer of the property's value. I put these items at the front of the *pro forma* because they are usually the first things an investor wants to see.

Next comes the property data sheet (Figure 10–3) you completed during your meeting with the seller. Note how detailed this property description is, naming the amenities and listing the total number of units that contain them. For instance, under property data you'll see that all 28 units have disposals, refrigerators, ranges, drapes and carpets. However, only 21 units have dishwashers. In this building the two- and three-bedroom units have dishwashers, while the seven one-bedroom units do not—a commonly encountered arrangement.

In the lower portion of the page the unit mix and rent schedule shows projected *market* rents as well as the current rents generated by the building. This is very important, especially when—as in our example—current rents are below prevailing market levels. This set of figures tells your buyer he or she can raise rents to bring them in line with those of comparable properties.

This is a good place to stress once again the importance of providing your client with maximum information about a building. Facts, facts, facts. The more the client has, the more easily he or she can make an intelligent investment decision concerning the purchase of the property.

If you have property data sheet categories for which you may not have precise facts, say so. Note, for example, the asterisk after net rentable sq. ft., relating to the phrase, "*Measurements are approximate." This caveat protects you in case someone else measures the area right down to a square millimeter.

The next page of the information *pro forma* package (Figure 10–4) is the completed income and expense summary that you also obtained at your meeting with the seller. Be sure to show projected rents based on your rental survey information and make adjustments in the projected expense column for any increases in costs that the new buyer may anticipate. In this example, higher estimates have been made for property taxes, insurance and maintenance. Indicate "Not Applicable" in categories that do not apply to the building with which you are working. For instance, in many properties owners do not employ the services of a professional management company.

The final page of the *pro forma* (Figure 10–5) provides the buyer with an overall investment analysis of the property. This information shows the cash flow, taxable income (or loss) and the projected property value of the building over a three-year period. Space is also provided to add any additional comments you may want to make. To determine the projections for the second and third years after purchase, certain assumptions regarding increases in rents and expenses must be made. In this example five-percent increases have been projected. Obviously, you will have to base your figures on the level of increases anticipated in your marketplace. For consistency in projecting future values, assume the same gross rent multiplier or cap rate that you determined appropriate at the time of purchase. For example, if your comparable sales data showed the market rate GRM to be 7.8 at the time of sale, multiply second- and third-year gross incomes by that number to determine the predicted property value for those years.

Preparing a *pro forma* makes you look like a true professional to all parties who will see your work—the buyer, seller and other real estate agents. Your clients will greatly appreciate getting information in a clean, well-organized presentation. The better job you do in setting forth the facts, the better your opportunity to make a sale.

(*Time-saving tip:* Type a master of the *pro forma* sheets, leaving spaces for inserting information. Copy these forms as you need them and simply fill in the blanks. The whole point of this book is not only to help you gain a rewarding career in selling apartments, but also to show you how to do things easily and quickly.)

Now that you have prepared your *pro forma*, you're ready to present your information package to your potential buyer. If, for some reason, your buyer doesn't purchase the apartment building, you have an ace in the hole. Your package is available for distribution to other investors or brokers.

Call your buyer and tell him or her that you've located an apartment property that suits the buyer's requirements. Ask for an appointment to present the facts in person. (*Reminder:* Don't reveal too much over the phone. If the buyer persists in asking for details like price, down payment, terms and so forth, you can simply say, ''I'm putting together all that information for you, and I'll be able to show you all the facts and figures when we get together.'' The one thing you *do* want to tell your client is the location of the apartment property. Try to arrange to visit the property with the buyer and then plan to present your detailed information immediately thereafter. Schedule a meeting in your office or, if the buyer prefers, in his or her office. Always try to avoid a meeting at the buyer's home. A residence can be a distracting environment.)

Most important, keep things moving along. ''Time is of the essence'' is a wise axiom for successful real estate transactions. When you phone the buyer about the property, try to convey a sense of urgency, without sounding anxious or desperate. Say something like, ''Mr. Buyer, I've located an apartment property that seems to be just what you're looking for. I think it will move pretty fast, and I want you to have the first opportunity to look it over. Could we get together today?''

When you have your appointment locked in, start practicing the key motto: *Be prepared.* Gather together *all* the information you will need—the *pro forma*, sales comparables, rental surveys and anything else of value that will help you back up your presentation of the property.

Above all, think ahead. Put yourself in the buyer's place. Consider objections he or she may raise and questions he or she may ask. Run a make-believe dialog through your mind. Plan your strategy for every possible twist and turn the conversation may take. It pays to anticipate your buyer's response to the presentation you're going to make. Think of it as a game, with *you* the winner of a big commission. Bear in mind, too, that the better prepared you are, the better you can serve both the buyer and the seller. That way, all three of you win.

If you've done things correctly up to this point, getting the buyer to make an offer should not be difficult. Doing things correctly means you have taken the following steps *before* you present the property information to your buyer: (1) matched the right buyer with the right property. Showing the investor something totally different from what he or she wants—unless it's an incredibly good deal—simply wastes everyone's time; (2) made sure you've determined the price of the building accurately and convinced the seller to market the property at that price; (3) collected factual data to support your statements and projections concerning the property.

When you meet with the buyer, do a thorough job of presenting and explaining the information about the property. Walk him through your *pro forma* step-by-step and answer questions as they arise. Don't rush through your presentation or skip over details. Take your time and make sure the buyer fully understands the proposed transaction. However, be careful not to let the conversation drift into irrelevant areas. Keep things on track and you'll be all set to write an offer.

STRUCTURING THE OFFER

When is it time to write an offer? When you sense that the buyer appears ready. Just follow the signs. Maybe the buyer nods his head in agreement with basic points in the *pro forma*. Perhaps he'll ask questions that tell you he's picturing owning the property. Watch his body language and listen to the tone of his voice. We all have a degree of intuition, and that amazing faculty seems to become stronger with practice. After a few presentations to buyers, you'll probably swear you're psychic! At the start, however, you may not pick up the signals automatically. Or this buyer may not be sending any.

If you do not detect signs that the buyer is ready, take the lead yourself. Briefly summarize all of buyer's decision-making criteria that the building satisfies and suggest a price at which he should make an offer. For instance, you might say something like this:

> Mr. Buyer, this is an exceptional property and represents an excellent value. The building appears to have all of the characteristics that you are looking for. It's the right size and unit mix and it's in the area you want. It's well maintained and close to shopping and public transportation. Why don't you make an offer of $XXX,XXX that I can take to the owner?

If you have convinced the seller to price the building fairly to begin with, you should suggest an initial offer as close to the asking price as possible, but with some room for negotiation. In the previous chapter I suggested leaving some bargaining space for the seller, too, when you priced the property. Allowing latitude for negotiating the price will help facilitate the sale in several ways.

Most buyers feel more comfortable making an offer somewhere below the asking price. Even if they end up paying close to the full price, they will want to test the seller with a lower offer to assure themselves that they have made the best deal possible. This process serves an important psychological function. If the buyer feels that he or she has purchased the property at the lowest price acceptable to the seller, it will help preclude unnerving and risky buyer's remorse later in the transaction. Also, by having some ability to raise his or her offer, the buyer will feel that he or she might be able to gain some concessions from the seller on other points, such as more favorable financing terms or a more desirable closing date. Offering a purchase price below the asking price also gives you a valuable psychological advantage in dealing with the seller. If the buyer immediately meets the full asking price, the seller may believe that he or she can obtain still more for the property. This is particularly dangerous if you don't have a signed listing with a stated asking figure. What is to prevent the seller from raising the price, perhaps to a sky-high level? This phenomenon is known as either greed or shrewd business sense, depending on how you view humanity.

On the other side of the picture, you should always discourage ridiculous "low-ball" offers from buyers. Presenting an absurdly low offer will only waste your time and damage your credibility with the seller. Therefore, an offer of from five percent to ten percent under the asking price is a good place to start. Such an offer is close enough to be realistic while still allowing room for negotiation. The desired end result will have the buyer coming up a little in price and the seller lowering the price a little, with both arriving at the fair market value of the property. The two parties will also feel that they have received something worthwhile from the other, thus attaining a most favorable deal for themselves.

A word of advice: As I have mentioned before, by using the special system explained in this book you will often be both the listing *and* the selling agent in many of your transactions. This dual role has the obvious benefit of enabling you to earn both sides of the commission. However, the extra commission dollars also bring added responsibility because you will be required to represent the best interests of both parties in these situations. Make sure you are familiar with all laws and regulations regarding the role of a dual agent in the state in which you will be conducting business. In the example that we discussed above, you could be required to inform the seller that the buyer may be willing to raise his or her offering price. It is imperative that you always operate legally and ethically, consistently adhering to the highest standards of integrity.

Once the buyer shows interest in buying the property, you should be the person to draw up the offer. If your buyer wants to talk with his or her CPA or attorney before making an offer, ask to be present at the meeting. Make sure the CPA and attorney consult only on tax and legal matters concerning the transaction and not on the property's price or investment potential. That is your domain. By allowing people in other professions to give advice on the economic merits of the real estate purchase, you could not only lose a sale, you could weaken your stature at the same time. Furthermore, you would be abdicating your proper role as an apartment sales specialist.

Standard contracts used for the purchase of real estate can vary greatly from state to state. If you have your real estate license or are studying for one, you should be familiar with the contracts used in your area. If not, consult your broker or instructor for clarification about these necessary documents. You don't have to be an attorney to deal with purchase contracts, but you should understand their basic legal aspects. Because of the diversity of contract forms, it is impossible to examine an entire purchase contract in this book. However, we can take a look at specific items that most apartment purchase contracts have in common.

Purchase contracts serve three basic purposes: (1) to fully state the details of the transaction to which each party can subscribe; (2) to provide for a timely and accurately described closing process (controlled by the broker) and (3) to minimize or prevent the possibility that either party can violate the contract. The purchase agreement is extremely important and calls for absolute accuracy. All such contracts should be typed, not handwritten. The contract should be worded so clearly that it cannot be misunderstood. The agreement should also be concise, with no cumbersome language or unnecessary repetition. The purchase price should be precisely stated with terms explicitly spelled out.

CONTINGENCIES

Contingencies (specific provisions) state that a contract is void or voidable on the occurrence (or nonoccurrence) of a particular happening. Every offer to purchase an apartment building will normally have certain contingencies inherent in such transactions. Contract contingencies should be reasonable both in character and in the time allowed for resolving them. You would be wise not to write purchase offers with immoderate contingencies. If the seller thinks the contingencies are too tough, he or she may suspect that the buyer is not very serious about purchasing the property and will be less inclined to accept the offer. Make it a rule to keep contingencies rational and hold them to a minimum number. Why place extra rocks in your path?

A major contingency in almost every real estate contract is the contingency to obtain financing. When writing the loan contingency, spell out the specific financing provisions that the buyer is seeking. These should include the loan amount, interest rate, length of term and financing costs. Also, be sure to give the buyer an adequate time frame in which to obtain the required financing commitment. Providing only 30 days to receive loan approval in a tight money market, for example, might be unrealistic.

The following are some additional contingencies common to apartment transactions:

> 1. "This offer is subject to Buyer's inspection and written approval or disapproval of all apartment interiors and exteriors situated on the herein described property within _____ days of Seller's acceptance of this offer."

Unlike a house sale, in apartment transactions the buyer usually does not inspect the interiors until after he or she has made an acceptable offer. A practical reason exists for the delayed inspection. If every interested (or curious) party could tour the units without making a written offer, such intrusions by unqualified visitors would be a tremendous inconvenience to tenants and the resident manager. Therefore, the apartment inspection is written as a contingency and is conducted after the acceptance of the offer.

The interior inspection is very important because sometimes an attractive exterior hides interior problems. For instance, maintenance of certain items may have been deferred for so long that repairs and replacements could cost a sizable sum.

If the buyer is not satisfied with the condition of the units after the inspection, he or she can attempt to renegotiate the deal or cancel the contract altogether. Circumstances specific to a transaction will dictate how long the buyer should have to inspect the building interior. However, 7 to 14 days is a suitable period of time for the buyer to remove this contingency.

In Chapter 12, I'll show you how to conduct an inspection of an apartment building inside and out.

> 2. "This offer is subject to Buyer's inspection and written approval or disapproval of the current rent schedule, all tenant rental agreements, and any and all contracts affecting the building, within _____ days of their receipt from Seller. Seller agrees to provide said items to Buyer within _____ days of Seller's acceptance of this offer."

This contingency allows the buyer to verify the rental rates provided in your property information package and to review the conditions of the tenant rental agreements and the terms of any contracts for services to which he or she might be obligated if he or she purchases the property. Ordinarily, the seller should provide this information within seven days of acceptance and the buyer should remove the contingency within seven days of the receipt of this information.

This is another significant contingency. For instance, a buyer who plans to raise under-market rents to prevailing levels might discover that the tenants have one-year leases that preclude rent increases until the end of the lease term. Or, the buyer may want to hire a landscape maintenance firm at a rate lower than that being paid by the current owner. Thus, it would be important to know the status of the existing service contracts.

> 3. "This offer is subject to Buyer's review and written approval or disapproval of the books and records for the previous 12 months of the subject property within _____ days of their receipt from Seller. Seller agrees to provide said items to Buyer within _____ days of his acceptance of this offer."

This contingency allows the buyer to inspect the property's actual income and expense statements. By doing so, he can verify and/or spot any irregularities in expenditures, rental rates and vacancies. These records will also show the average length of tenancy for the apartments. The time frame for the satisfaction of this contingency is normally the same as for the preceding contingency (number 2).

> 4. "Included in the purchase price is all personal property used in operation of the premises, including, but not limited to, all drapes, wall-to-wall carpeting, appliances and furniture belonging to Seller. Seller shall deliver a complete inventory to Buyer within _____ days of Seller's acceptance of this offer. Buyer to provide written approval or disapproval of said inventory within _____ days of its receipt from Seller."

This contingency allows for clarification of what personal property used in the operation of the complex is or isn't included in the sale of the building. The time period for removing this contingency should be the same as for numbers 2 and 3.

Before we move on to the next section, let me add a note about "termite clearances." In the sale of a single-family residence a termite clearance is usually a standard contingency in almost every contract, with the responsibility for any corrective work placed squarely on the seller's shoulders. However, in apartment sales a termite clearance is usually a completely negotiable item between buyer and seller. There are several reasons for this. First, in the sale of a house, a termite clearance is normally required by the lender, which is not typically the case in the sale of an apartment building. Second, because of the size of an apartment building, the cost of corrective work can be very expensive and an owner ordinarily would not leave himself blindly open to such a major expense by guaranteeing a termite clearance. Also, it is extremely difficult, or at least impractical, to coordinate the temporary relocation of the tenants during chemical fumigation if the termite situation requires extensive treatment and repair. However, since the buyer will want to know the condition of the building, the seller will usually provide the buyer with a certified termite report describing any damage due to infestation. As I said earlier, the responsibility for correcting a termite problem will become an item for negotiation.

CLAUSES AND CONDITIONS

Besides the basic contingencies we've just reviewed, there are also some clauses and conditions that are usually part of an offer to purchase an apartment building. Two such provisions are:

1. "Seller shall deliver title to all personal property by Bill of Sale free and clear from all liens and encumbrances." Upon the closing of the transaction, a grant deed will convey title to the *real* property and a bill of sale should be used to convey title to the *personal* property that is to be included in the sale.

2. "Any and all deposits, including, but not limited to, security deposits, key deposits, cleaning deposits and pet deposits deposited by tenants, shall be turned over to the Buyer by the Seller through escrow." This condition helps ensure the proper transfer of all tenant deposits from the seller to the buyer at the close of the transaction.

As noted at the beginning of this section, contracts vary in form and content and it is impossible to cover every contingency that may be needed in a given situation. Consider the preceding examples of contingencies, clauses and conditions as guides to common contract inclusions that you can expect to use in an apartment purchase offer.

PRESENTING THE OFFER

Ready? Your first sale can be just a short distance away now!

You are about to complete the circle and return to your seller with a purchase offer. The basic rules of presenting the offer are similar to those that you followed in helping your buyer make the offer in the first place—but with a few differences. Following these guidelines will pay off for you.

As soon as you have the signed purchase offer from your buyer, phone the seller for an appointment. Again, time is a critical element, so get moving right away. And what are those two magic words again? You've got it: *Be prepared.* If I repeat that phrase, it's because advance preparation is absolutely essential to every single apartment property sale you will make.

When you call the seller, he or she will want to know all about the offer. But don't reveal any details by phone. As you did with the buyer, make an appointment to deliver the offer in person. *Tip:* If you have a secretary or other assistant, ask him or her to phone the seller and make the appointment for you. A property owner probably won't ask a secretary for details of the offer. If the owner is persistent, your secretary can simply explain that only you have all the necessary information. Besides, if the secretary doesn't have a real estate license, he or she cannot legally discuss the deal anyway. As with the buyer, try to meet the seller in your office or, as a second choice, in his or her office. A businesslike environment—instead of a living room or cocktail lounge—will enhance your discussion and make it more productive. Be cordial during your meeting to make the seller feel comfortable, but maintain a professional approach.

When you present the offer, do it slowly and methodically. Start by giving the seller background information about the buyer. It will be important for you to be able to honestly assure the seller that the potential purchaser is qualified and able to close the deal. The more solid your buyer sounds, the better his or her offer will look. You can increase the likelihood of having the offer accepted if the seller feels there's a high probability that the deal will close. Therefore, be certain that you know as much as possible about your buyer. Continue your presentation by explaining all details of the contract including the price and terms offered by the buyer, contingencies that will need to be satisfied, the closing date, and other main points. Be sure that the seller fully understands the entire offer and be ready to give thorough answers to any questions he or she may have.

If you are fortunate enough to have the seller accept the offer as presented, give him a handshake, congratulate him on his good business decision and assure him that you'll follow through on all details of the transaction. Then wind up the meeting and leave. Don't linger on with cocktails and conversation. Believe it or not, at this point you both could socialize yourselves right out of the sale. Take a hint from the top salespeople: When you've made the sale, stop talking about it.

Most likely, though, there will always be some items of disagreement that will need to be negotiated and resolved before the contract is totally acceptable to both parties.

So sit tight, the game isn't over yet. In the next chapter, I'll give you some tips on ways to overcome buyer and seller differences and put the opposing players together on the same team.

SUMMING UP WHAT YOU'VE LEARNED IN CHAPTER 10

Your degree of professionalism shows in the way you present an apartment property to a qualified buyer. You'll be at your best when you adhere to these basic points.

1. Prepare a *pro forma* property description as shown in this chapter to present an apartment property to a prospective buyer or other agents. Make this property profile complete in every detail.

2. Walk your buyer through every item on the *pro forma* presentation and answer all questions thoroughly.

3. *You* should write the offer. The buyer's CPA and attorney should be involved in accounting and legal counsel only, *not* in judging the value of the purchase.

4. Keep contingencies (provisions and conditions) to an absolute minimum.

5. When you have a signed purchase offer, immediately call the seller for an appointment. Don't give details of the offer by phone.

6. As soon as the purchase offer is accepted, don't linger with conversation. You could talk yourself out of a sale.

7. Represent *both* buyer and seller equally and fairly.

CHAPTER **11**

Negotiating the Sale

"Let us never negotiate out of fear,
but let us never fear to negotiate."

—JOHN F. KENNEDY

If everyone always agreed with everyone else on every subject, life would be very simple. And a little boring. But you won't have to fight off yawns in your apartment sales career because there are few dull moments when putting buyers and sellers together.

Yes, sometimes, miracles can happen. You could encounter a buyer so eager to own a certain apartment building that he or she might readily pay the full asking price and meet all the terms and conditions demanded by the seller. Or you might find a financially distressed owner desperate enough to accept almost any offer. But don't count on things like that happening often.

Virtually every apartment transaction requires some degree of give and take. And because both buyer and seller seem to believe it is better to receive than to give, each wants to gain the most and sacrifice the least.

That is why it is important for us to take time in this chapter to review some basic negotiating techniques that will help you resolve buyer-seller differences and bring both parties together with a mutually acceptable sales contract. Look at negotiating as a game (which it is). If you play it smart, everyone wins. The buyer and seller will have an agreement that satisfies both parties and you'll be a big step closer to depositing a nice commission check.

Don't let the thought of negotiating an apartment sale intimidate you because you'll have a big advantage in bringing everyone and everything together. And that advantage is the system you are learning in this book. I say that with total confidence because I have developed, tested and *proven* these special tech-

niques with the sole purpose of reducing the amount of negotiations required to the lowest level possible. Throughout this book
I have stressed the necessity of working only on transactions that
have a high probability of closing. Let me advise you once again
to avoid dealing with clients whose expectations of the marketplace are totally unrealistic. Although there will be some gaps
to bridge in almost every transaction, no amount of negotiating
will help sell an apartment building whose owner is convinced
his or her property is worth more than the market dictates. Nor
will the most skillful negotiating help consummate a transaction
when your prospective buyer is looking only for an absolute
"steal." If, however, you work solely with qualified and motivated buyers and sellers on properties that are priced according
to market values, you should have the respective parties close
to an agreement at the beginning of the deal. Then, whatever
differences exist can easily be resolved.

OFFER AND COUNTEROFFER

In the preceding chapter we prepared the offer from the buyer
and presented it to the seller. We also discussed what steps to
take when you're fortunate enough to have the owner accept the
offer as written. However, as I'm sure you're aware, in a normal
transaction the buyer usually has offered less than the asking
price. And, most likely, several other items will have to be
resolved before the contract can be approved by both parties.

Now is when you'll begin to learn the meaning of "shuttle
diplomacy" as you move back and forth between buyer and seller
with offer and counteroffer, steadily narrowing the distance
between their respective positions until all gaps have been closed.
Don't let this part of the transaction process disturb you. If Henry
Kissinger can do it, so can you! You're over the hump at this point
and you're getting down to dotting the i's and crossing the t's.
Just keep your wits and keep a vision of that king-sized commission in the front of your mind and you'll do just fine.

KNOWING YOUR ROLE

The buyer and seller must always recognize and respect you as
the mediator. Once again, here is where your stature as a profes-

sional counts. In your very first meetings with the buyer and seller, get things off to the right start by demonstrating to both parties that you are a sincere, knowledgeable and earnest person in whom they can have full confidence. Maintain a high level of enthusiasm at all times and convey to the buyer and seller your belief that the needs of both parties will be served and that the sale will go through. If you are upbeat about the property and the prospects for a successful sale, both buyer and seller will find it easier to trust the advice and direction you offer. In all negotiations—from apartment transactions to international relations—the optimism and energy of the mediator can set the stage for agreement.

Be sure that everyone—including you—keeps the negotiating process in proper prospective. Simply tossing numbers back and forth between the two parties will not always resolve all the differences in a given transaction. Even though they probably have never met, the parties tend to perceive each other as adversaries. Your success as mediator will be greatly enhanced when you can reverse those attitudes and have buyer and seller viewing each other as compatible people working toward a common goal.

You can do several things to bring about a meeting of the minds. In every transaction some items will be negotiable and others will be virtually chiseled in granite. Therefore, the first step is to determine those points on which one or both parties may be flexible. Since each party wants to gain something from the other, you can see the importance of knowing which positions can be bent one way or another.

When one party yields on a certain point in the contract, you can show the other party where he will gain. In so doing, you will be able to present the counteroffer in a positive light because you can demonstrate how various concessions can bring both parties closer together. Such a demonstration is important because many investors tend to view a counteroffer as a rejection of the original proposal instead of as a compromise or alternative approach. By pointing out the positive aspects of the negotiation process, you can help prevent a client from immediately attacking the counteroffer in an effort to defend his or her original proposal. Convince the buyer and seller that the best way for each to gain as much as possible is to give up considerations that are secondary to the main objective. By telling each party the concessions the other is willing to make, you can more easily convince both parties that each side is acting in a fair and willing manner.

When either party does make a concession during the negotiations, reinforce his commitment to it by diplomatically complimenting him for his intelligent decision. Make sure, though, that you match the amount of praise to the size of the concession.

HOW TO MAINTAIN CONTROL

It is essential to the success of the sale that *you* control the negotiations at all times. This is important for a couple of reasons. By being in the driver's seat, you can keep the negotiations on the most direct route to a sale. If you let the buyer or the seller assume too strong a role, the bargaining can take wasteful twists and turns. If that happens, you'll spend most of your time trying to even things out again and you could be unjustly perceived as favoring one party or another. Also, as the guiding force in the negotiations, you'll have the maneuverability you need to propose solutions to difficulties that may arise as matters proceed.

Let's take a look at several means by which you can maintain control of the negotiating process.

Plan Ahead.   Before you meet with a buyer or seller to conduct negotiations, develop a plan for the conference. Size up the situation carefully and be sure you fully understand the items that are to be discussed. Play out a little drama in your mind, hearing and seeing yourself setting forth the contract content plainly and concisely. If you ramble and do not present the issues clearly, the meeting can drift and your client will lose interest in the discussion. You may also open the door for the client to usurp your leadership position. Anticipate the objections the buyer or seller may raise about the points you present and develop strategies to help overcome them. Prepare any supporting information that you feel will help both parties cooperate in reaching an agreement. Even though all three of you speak the same language, you will be a sort of interpreter—explaining or justifying the stance of one party and often restating the view of the other party so that each will see the other's perspective. Your moderator role is especially important when you are dealing with people who tend to be highly demanding or intransigent. Refresh your memory about the motivations of both the buyer and seller and, if the negotiations stray off course, remind each party of these basic positive factors to keep everyone focused on the goal of a successful sale.

The better you prepare yourself, the more relaxed and secure you will be when you talk to your clients. Your confidence and command of the situation will make it easier for your clients to be guided by you.

Choose the Setting.   The same rules apply here as when you presented the purchase offer. Try to conduct negotiations in a business environment. Your office is always the best place to negotiate because you will tend to perform better on your own turf. Also, clients who come to your office are inclined to be more receptive and compliant because, in a very real sense, they are your guests, and guests usually like to be on their best behavior.

However, if you must meet the client at his or her home, do your best to find a quiet setting for the meeting so that everyone can concentrate on the tasks at hand. If the client's kids are playing World War III and the TV is going full blast, suggest moving to a less noisy part of the house. A proper environment helps maintain everyone's interest and allows you to keep the discussions channeled in the right direction.

Learn to Listen.   You might think that this is an easy job. And it should be. However, many salespeople are so engrossed in formulating what they are going to say next that they fail to grasp what the other party is trying to tell them. Being a good listener is more than just *hearing* words that someone is speaking. You must be able to concentrate on what is being said and how it is being stated so that you can *understand* not just the words themselves but the meaning of their message. Elementary? Yes, but intelligent listening is too often neglected. The quality of your response will improve remarkably when you begin to focus on the other person's words *first*.

At all times display interest in what the other person is saying. If your client senses that you are not paying attention, he or she may become quiet, impatient, bored or downright agitated, quickly dissipating your control of the situation. Without simply repeating what the other person says, reply in a manner that lets the client know that you comprehend and thoughtfully consider what was just said. Maintain eye contact and respond to the other party appropriately in speech or gesture, but do not interrupt unless it's totally warranted.

Incorporate these tips into your everyday conversations and work to become a better listener. When you meet with buyers and sellers you will find that attentive listening skills greatly enhance your effectiveness as a negotiator.

Take the Initiative. Be assertive and present ideas that will help point the negotiations in the direction you want them to go. It is particularly important that you do so when the buyer or seller has no clear-cut thoughts about how the transaction should progress. The earlier you assume a position of leadership in the negotiating process, the easier it will be for you to retain and strengthen your control of the give-and-take procedure leading to a closed deal.

Use Suggestive Questions. Often you can guide your clients into making decisions by using leading or suggestive questions that start them thinking about ways to settle their temporary differences. If the buyer is hanging tough on a certain price, a "what if" question could help. "What if you would carry back a little more of the loan"? you might ask the seller. Or, you may be dealing with a buyer who is adamantly resisting a certain interest rate the seller wants in return for carrying back some of the financing. "What if the seller would extend the term of his secondary loan to give you a lower monthly payment"? you could inquire. Having asked some leading questions, you could then say to both the buyer and the seller, "Of course, you probably have some good ideas of your own on how to resolve this matter." No one likes to admit that he or she doesn't have a single idea in his or her head. Pride will often lead either party—or both—to suggest a solution, if only to prove how wise and fair he or she is. Using this technique, you avoid making the decision yourself and then trying to force the client into accepting it. Also, when a client feels that he or she has made a decision, he or she will be more committed to the choice throughout the transaction.

Sometimes, too, it helps to ask a rhetorical question—one that is asked only for effect and requires no answer. An example is, "I really don't believe there is any situation that cannot somehow be resolved, do you?" You don't need a reply to that one because who is going to concede that he or she is permanently stopped cold by a problem that could be sensibly negotiated?

Don't Promise What You Can't Deliver.   The only person that you can absolutely speak for in a deal is yourself. Therefore, when negotiating with buyers and sellers, promise *only* what you are totally responsible for and can deliver with 100 percent certainty. Never guarantee anything on behalf of one party or the other unless that person has previously consented to it, preferably in writing.

Many agents make the mistake of getting so caught up in the excitement of concluding a sale that they promise certain concessions or agreements before consulting the responsible party. For instance, a deal may be close at hand on an $800,000 apartment building and the buyer says, "I'll go along with everything else if the seller will reduce his price by $5,000." The agent, believing that $5,000 is a small amount when compared to the purchase price says, "That shouldn't be a problem with the seller. I think we have a deal." He then goes to the seller only to learn that a $5,000 reduction in price *is* a big problem and the seller will not agree to it. Not only does the agent now look foolish to the buyer, but his credibility is lost and he will be operating from a position of weakness throughout the remainder of the negotiating process.

No matter how small the client's demand may seem, your best strategy is to respond that you will present the request to the other party and do your best to obtain a favorable reply.

Set Time Limits to Resolve Differences.   Remember, time is *always* a key factor in any real estate transaction. To be a successful negotiator you—as the mediator—must set reasonable time limits in which to resolve differences between the buyer and seller. Then, do your best to keep the negotiations on schedule. Deals that are left to linger with no time constraints for the resolution of disagreements will quickly fall apart. A myriad of deal killers are always waiting to raise their ugly heads whenever time is allowed to plod on unrestricted. If the seller is slow to respond, for instance, the buyer could become annoyed with the seller's inertia and look for another property. If the opposite is true, the seller could develop second thoughts about selling the property and take it off the market. Whatever the reason for the delay, your chances of successfully consummating the sale will be in serious jeopardy if you fail to establish time limits.

Be Concise and Productive. When meeting with buyers and sellers, keep the negotiating discussions as brief and productive as possible. If you let the sessions drag on, the client may want to rehash items that you thought you had previously resolved. Prepare properly for the meeting and have specific objectives that you want to achieve. When you have met your aims, end the meeting and move on to the next segment of the transaction.

Don't Oversell. Once you have convinced a client to agree to a certain item, avoid the mistake of overselling the point. Quickly move on to another area that needs discussion, or conclude the meeting altogether if that was the only item that needed to be cleared up during the session. Many agents make the mistake of continuing to discuss particular aspects of a contact even after those points have been resolved. Sometimes they belabor the issue because the client agreed to certain points faster than anticipated or because the agent wants to make sure he really heard a yes. Don't press your luck. The time immediately following the "consent" is crucial. If you persist in discussing the issue, you could actually raise new questions that might alter the previous positive decision.

Keep Buyers and Sellers Apart. Yes, you read it correctly. With few exceptions, do *not* introduce the buyer and the seller to each other during the negotiating process. This important rule derives from sound reasoning. If the buyer and seller meet before an acceptable agreement has been reached, you could have some troublesome problems on your hands. With the parties dealing face-to-face, your role as mediator will be largely diminished, along with a great measure of the control that you should be exerting on the situation. You will have a much harder time offering suggestions without seeming to favor one side or the other. Also, without a buffer (you) between the principals, egos have a way of entering the scene, with one party trying to outdo the other through personal power ploys. If one party has the stronger personality, he or she may seem pushy or intimidating to the other. Perhaps the problem will be only a matter of chemistry with the two disliking each other. In any event, since one will be trying to obtain something from the other, they will be in adversarial positions and it is best to keep them apart.

Be Yourself.   You will always be at your best when you are truly being yourself. Incorporate the preceding suggestions into your sales repertoire and, at the same time, concentrate on putting your own personality into the negotiating process. Don't put on a different face for each party in the transaction. You may want to adjust your level of intensity to fit the situation, but the person showing up as the negotiating agent should always be the real *you*. When Shakespeare had Polonius advise Laertes in *Hamlet*, ''This above all—to thine own self be true,'' the playwright knew what he was talking about.

BREAKING A DEADLOCK

What if negotiations reach a total impasse? This can and does happen, especially if an apartment sale transaction continues over a considerable period of time. Sometimes either the seller, the buyer—or both—gets so bogged down in side issues or irrelevant details that the prime goal of concluding the sale becomes lost. When a deadlock occurs, you'll once again realize the importance of controlling the situation. *Take charge immediately!*

You may have to call a temporary halt to the stymied negotiations and suggest that both parties stand back and take a fresh look at the whole matter. Review with each of them the progress they've made and the differences they've resolved. Be positive and encouraging by showing the two parties how close together they already are to reaching an agreement. Suggest holding a meeting two or three days later to let the dust settle.

Then, get busy. Write a summary of where the deal stands at the moment. Do some thinking about new negotiating possibilities. This can actually be a fun part of the process for you because you have full freedom to be creative. You'll perhaps recall a certain comment the buyer made or an almost forgotten statement made by the seller. Suddenly, the light will flash and you'll have a new perspective on the situation or a new offer to suggest to your buyer or seller. Talk to your associates and other brokers. Their experience with a buyer-seller deadlock may give you exactly the idea you're looking for.

Next, set up separate meetings with the buyer and seller as soon as possible. Show each one your written summary of the status of negotiations and make your new suggestions for a compromise. This action on your part will provide two important advantages. First, you can point to the number of concessions already made by both parties. Doing so is psychologically valuable because people tend to become more flexible in their position when they see, in black on white, how much the other party has surrendered. They also see that *their* concessions have greatly helped to move the negotiations forward. When both parties realize how close they are to the mutually desired goal, the transaction will pick up speed. Second, this updated summary provides a fresh starting point for reaching a final agreement. Thus, you have a platform for presenting your new suggestions that can bring the negotiations to a successful conclusion.

If you still encounter a stalemate, don't be afraid to make a bold move. In a friendly but direct way, tell the more intractable party that the other party may not be willing to continue the negotiations much longer. Diplomatically explain that the buyer (or the seller) definitely wants to conclude a deal and will probably start looking for another seller (or buyer). Express your honest conviction that the ongoing negotiations can lead to an excellent transaction and that you are willing to do whatever is necessary to consummate the sale. Plain talk such as that can often move a stalled deal off dead center, making your work pay off. The buyer and seller will also feel compelled to respect your frank statement because they will have to recognize it as the truth.

THE RULE OF FAIRNESS

It's a basic truth that has been proven time and again: Negotiations move along smoothly as long as the goal of *fairness* wins out over individual motivations. This "rule of fairness," as it is called by professional negotiators for the State Department, corporations and labor organizations, applies to all pacts reached by mutual agreement—including apartment transactions. Behavioral scientists have demonstrated the fact that all normal humans—regardless of their differences and faults—accept a concept of fairness because it represents a state of equilibrium. This is a formal way of saying that people breathe a sigh of relief when they reach an agreement with others. We all like to feel that everything is somehow in balance and that all is right with the world.

You can help bring about that happy result by being totally *fair* with both the buyer and the seller. Try to see each negotiating item from both points of view and be honest in your appraisal of how the deal is progressing. Whenever you can improve the situation, do so without hesitation.

As I've pointed out in other areas of this book, your integrity is *all*-important. Remember, you're not merely making a single sale. You're making or breaking your reputation based on how you handle yourself and how well you serve the valid interests of your clients.

In the next chapter, I'll show you how to conduct an on-site inspection of an apartment property and place your sale into escrow.

SUMMING UP WHAT YOU'VE LEARNED
IN CHAPTER 11

Negotiating is the art of compromise. It is the process of making all parties feel that they have received the best part of the deal. These pointers will make your clients happy and you a hero.

1. Establish credibility and trust with your clients by demonstrating sincerity and impartiality.

2. Handle offers and counteroffers in writing, in person and immediately.

3. Keep the buyer and seller apart. Ideally, they shouldn't meet face-to-face until the deal closes.

4. Maintain *control* of negotiations at all times.

5. Mentally put yourself in the place of the buyer and seller. Seeing both sides clearly hastens an agreement.

6. Set time limits for resolving differences. Don't let things drag on and falter.

7. Keep negotiating sessions brief and productive.

8. To break a deadlock, call a brief halt to negotiations and use that time to develop new ideas for agreement.

9. Be enthusiastic and confident about a happy outcome. Optimism is a powerful factor in negotiations.

10. Be assertive and persistent in moving toward a closing.

CHAPTER 12

Closing the Deal

*"Education is hanging around
until you've caught on."*

—ROBERT FROST

Heads up! You're almost home. If you have done everything right so far, you're ready to perform the final steps before you collect your commission check.

Your path is clear and straight ahead if you've correctly followed all of the instructions described in previous chapters. You have learned your market, built your apartment catalog, made cold calls, put together a motivated buyer and seller, correctly priced the property and structured a tightly written, explicit offer. With all this working for you, your transaction will have an overwhelming probability of closing.

Once again, *time* is always an extremely important factor in your new career, especially now that you're so close to wrapping up the transaction. You are the agent that solidifies the ingredients of a sale. You are also the driving force that pushes the transaction to the only goal you should have: closing the deal. So keep things *moving*.

Even the smoothest running sales transaction can have a few glitches here and there, but they usually can be worked out. The key to success at this stage is to solve small problems quickly so that they don't turn into big troubles. Stay on top of everything. Don't expect the buyer or seller to carry things forward. They won't—out of sheer inertia if for no other reason. Cover every last detail. Don't be timid about pushing and prodding the people involved. Think ahead. Anticipate potential problems. If troubles do not crop up, at least you'll have been prepared to solve them. Take full responsibility for coordinating the entire transaction.

I repeat, take care of *all* details *immediately*. The less you do to move the deal along, the greater the chance of something going wrong. You want the commission check and, after all the good work you've done, you deserve it. Don't let it slip away.

OPENING ESCROW

In this chapter, for the sake of clarity, I will refer to the final stage of the transaction as *escrow,* the process by which a neutral third party acts on behalf of both the buyer and the seller in carrying out the instructions of those two parties and in disbursing the funds when all purchase agreement conditions have been met. In some states, methods other than escrow are used to transfer the ownership of property from one party to another. Your real estate license instructors, local brokers or title companies will explain the equivalent of escrow if this procedure is not used in your state.

The first step of this process is to choose an escrow officer to assist you in handling this last stage of the deal. But not just *any* escrow officer! Choose an escrow officer who is heavily experienced in handling *apartment* transactions and *only* such a specialist. I cannot make this point too emphatically: *Do not* entrust all your hard work and the interests of your buyer and seller to someone whose escrow experience is limited to dealing with houses and condos. By now you know that the apartment sales field is highly specialized and you can't afford the risk of jeopardizing your sale because someone doesn't understand all the intricacies of apartment escrows. You could not only end up with delays and frustration, but—worst of all—you might lose the entire sale. Apartment escrow experts, by contrast, can help you tremendously every step of the way. They can take things in stride, help you come up with ready solutions to problems and expedite the entire process. If you have not become acquainted earlier with an apartment escrow specialist, call other brokers or lenders and find out who is the best. You can't settle for less. It's that important.

The escrow officer will open the escrow by rewriting the terms and conditions of the purchase contract into the form of escrow instructions. Once you have the escrow instructions, get them to your buyer and seller for signature in a hurry. And always *hand-deliver all* documents. Do not trust the mail delivery. Carry the escrow instructions *in person* to the buyer and to the seller. Explain to each all details of the escrow instructions and answer any questions they may have. (*You'll* know the answers because you probably asked your escrow officer the same questions! That's why you're smart to deal with experts.)

REMOVING CONTINGENCIES

Now it's time to begin satisfying the contingencies to which the buyer and seller agreed in the sales contract. These will include the items discussed in Chapter 10, such as the on-site inspection, financing, review of books and records and other items, along with any additional contingencies that may be needed in a particular transaction.

Your first step in this process will be to schedule the date and time of the on-site inspection. This is usually within seven to ten days after the seller's acceptance of the offer. The purpose of this inspection is to assure the buyer that the building has no serious defects and that he is getting the value he expects based on the information provided by the seller and his impression of the property during the initial preview. If the on-site inspection reveals any discrepancies of previously unknown defects, adjustments in price can possibly be made with further negotiations, or the buyer can elect to cancel the transaction altogether.

To initiate the on-site inspection, the owner must first give notice to the tenants that an inspection of their apartment units will take place at a certain time on a specific date. Tenant laws can vary from state to state, but in many states tenants must be given written notice at least 24 hours in advance of the inspection. Be sure to familiarize yourself with the tenant laws in your area. Usually, you can get this information from your local apartment owners association or board of realtors.

Get the inspection ball rolling by advising the seller to prepare the needed number of copies of the notice of inspection and have them distributed to all tenants in the building. Usually, the notice will give no indication that the property is for sale and it may be signed by the resident manager rather than by the owner. Some tenants who are made aware of the fact that the apartment building is on the market might fear a rental increase and may make plans to move. Or just the uncertainty of what a new owner will be like can cause undue consternation throughout the building.

If tenants do raise questions concerning the inspection, they can be informed that the management is conducting a maintenance inspection for a new insurance policy, or that the owner is considering refinancing the building and the visitors will be potential lenders. Before you judge this as deception, bear in mind that it is necessary to keep things on an even keel during this important stage. A mass exodus of tenants could be disastrous. Remember, too, that tenants can often benefit by a sale if the new owner makes needed repairs and improvements to the building.

A typical letter to the tenants is shown below.

Dear Tenants:

At 10:00 a.m. on Wednesday, April 6, 1987, the management of this complex will be conducting an interior inspection of all apartment units. The inspection will be brief and we will be careful to disturb you as little as possible. Your cooperation is greatly appreciated.

Sincerely,

Fred Reynolds
Resident Manager

PLANNING THE INSPECTION

Meet with the buyer as soon as the inspection is scheduled and map out plans for the on-site tour. How extensive the inspection should be will depend on the age and condition of the building and the buyer's level of knowledge and sophistication. A building in obvious need of repair makes a thorough inspection mandatory. If you see extensive neglect in the exterior of the structure, deteriorating landscaping, chuck holes in the parking lot and other highly visible defects, you can be pretty sure that the interior won't win a beauty contest either. At the same time, a building in seemingly good shape on the outside can be hiding deferred maintenance problems on the inside.

An old hand at buying apartments will be able to anticipate most of the problem areas and will know what to look for and what kinds of inspectors, if any, he or she will want to bring with him for the inspection. A first-time buyer, however, may definitely want to have enough professionals at the inspection—plumbers, electricians or even a structural engineer—to assure himself that all possible problems will be found. At the same time, try to keep the inspection group to a manageable size. You don't want the inspection tour to look like a contractor's convention, a spectacle that would upset the tenants. Also, a large group inside an apartment makes the unit look small—a negative factor in the buyer's eyes. If, on the whole, the building is in good condition, a skilled and versatile handyman or a general contractor can ably cover several bases, such as checking out electrical and plumbing facilities, plus inspecting doors and cabinetry.

One area of the building definitely should be inspected by a professional: the roof. Sometimes even a brand-new roof is installed with such shoddy workmanship and poor materials that the first heavy rain can cause serious damage. Replacing an apartment building roof can cost thousands of dollars—a good reason for you to firmly recommend that the buyer order this indispensable inspection.

Tip: If a termite inspection is part of the purchase agreement, make sure it is scheduled for the same day as the on-site inspection. By coordinating the termite inspection with the overall building tour, you'll be able to avoid a second interruption of the tenants. Furthermore, if the termite inspection is delayed until later in the deal, sellers often resist a second inspection that could turn up hitherto unnoticed defects. Why give yourself problems? Get the termite inspection over and done with during the original on-site tour.

Work with your buyer, and contact the needed inspectors right away. If he procrastinates, nudge him along. Remember that vital time element again. You have only a short time until the inspection date rolls around and the trade professionals you will be using will need ample advance notification so that they can arrange their schedules. If the buyer is a novice, inform him that, with the possible exception of the termite report, it will be his responsibility to assume the costs of any professionals asked to perform an inspection.

One other word to the wise: It is better not to have the seller present during the on-site inspection. The buyer and his inspectors will be looking for any problems or defects and the seller is likely to become defensive if the experts turn up a trouble spot. The one thing you don't need is a confrontation between seller and buyer. In fact, as I pointed out in the previous chapter, the ideal situation is to avoid any kind of face-to-face meeting of buyer and seller until escrow closes. Again, I emphasize how important it is that *you* control the entire transaction, from start to finish.

Arrange to have the resident manager, not the seller, show you through the complex during the on-site inspection. This arrangement has definite advantages. The resident manager won't react as emotionally as the seller to the inspectors' pointing out problems because it isn't his building. Also, since the resident manager is normally aware that the building is for sale, he is likely to put his best foot forward in the new buyer's presence because he will probably want to keep his job after the sale. Furthermore, he can better answer questions about the tenants and the building since he is the one who spends the most time at the property. Thus, the resident manager can be of decided help during the on-site inspection.

Now you're ready for the inspection, but while you're waiting for the on-site tour to come about, have the seller gather together all necessary information so the buyer can review the data and begin removing other contingencies in the purchase offer. Such papers will include the rental agreements, operating statements (books and records), an inventory list, maintenance contracts and other items pertinent to the property and the sale. (Review ''Contingencies'' in Chapter 10.)

See what I mean about keeping things moving? It's easy to put several things in motion at the same time. Besides speeding up the transaction, you'll also be in continuous touch with both the seller and the buyer, thereby staying on top of any new developments on either side. Moreover, you're demonstrating to both parties that you are an energetic dedicated professional who knows how to get things done.

THE EXTERIOR INSPECTION

The on-site tour usually begins by walking the grounds and examining the exterior of the premises. The inspectors, the buyer and you will be checking, among other items, the condition of the building's outside walls, the parking lot, landscaping, swimming pool and pool filter system, water heaters, furnaces, air conditioners and the roof, which, as I noted earlier, should be inspected by a roofing specialist.

Figure 12–1, on page 171, shows an inspection form that you can take along to record the condition of the major exterior components of the apartment building. Under condition mark *E* (Excellent), *F* (Fair), or *P* (Poor). In the improvement column list any repairs you and the buyer feel a particular component may need, and enter the anticipated expense in the estimated cost column. Also, be sure to carry a legal-sized notepad for jotting down anything else that you may need to remember or discuss at the end of the inspection.

Next let's step into the interior of the units to complete our on-site inspection.

THE INTERIOR INSPECTION

Here's where you'll get the inside story of the apartment building. Impress on the buyer the importance of inspecting *every* apartment interior. The reason, of course, is that you must have a complete picture of the entire building. Suppose the buyer inspected only, say, eight out of 24 units. The carpet may be in fairly good condition in six or seven of those eight units, but might be torn, stained or burned in several of those you *didn't* inspect. If replacing the carpet in a unit costs, for instance, $700, replacing ruined carpet in just a few of the units would total several thousand dollars! Inspecting each unit takes just a few minutes, but the time spent doing so will be well worth it. Again, I suggest you tell the buyer that all units should be checked out. If he says that he is satisfied with seeing only a portion of the units, okay. He's the boss. But the *buyer* must make that decision. The point of your urging a total interior inspection is to protect yourself in the future. If, at a later date, the buyer complains that he didn't realize some of the units on the second floor were in terrible shape, you have sheltered yourself from liability in the situation.

For the interior inspection, you'll need a supply of two-page inspection reports, such as the sample in Figure 12–2. Take along enough of these forms so that you can fill out one for every apartment unit. The form is designed for quick easy use and completeness of content. Each sheet is identified with the apartment number and unit type (studio, one bedroom, two bedroom and so on). Fill out the form in the same manner as described previously for the exterior status report.

These reports, when completed, will provide a profile of each unit's condition. This way, you'll know the good points and problems in every unit so that it will be easy to review the facts with the buyer and the seller.

If any tenants are home at the time of the inspection, begin the tour of the unit by asking the tenants if everything in the apartment is working properly. This approach not only helps you quickly detect any problems, but also lets the tenants feel that you are interested in their satisfaction with the apartment. Good psychology pays off in their cooperation with your inspection visit.

Next, go right down your checklist on the inspection report and see for yourself how things work or don't work. Turn on the disposal. Open the refrigerator and freezer section. Look for leaky pipes under the kitchen cabinet sink. Turn on the range hood fan (one of the most frequent trouble spots). Check the bathroom sink for leaks and flush the toilet to make sure it functions as it should. Look at all ceilings for water marks that indicate a leaking roof. Inspect drapes for tears and stains. How's the carpet in the living room and other areas? Look for cracks or holes in the interior walls. Check all doors and work the locks.

Use the notes portion of the interior inspection report for other problems or observations. Maybe you'll note that the tenants in number 21 are rough people who have damaged the apartment and live in dirty conditions. The buyer may want them to move when he takes over. On the positive side, you may want to make a notation about an exceptionally clean apartment when you inspect it.

After the inspection is completed, sit down with the buyer over a cup of coffee or meet that evening and review the situation. *Don't wait.* Go over the inspection reports without delay, and help the buyer decide if there are any problems or discrepancies that he feels the seller should repair or replace before the close of escrow. Keep in mind that the purpose of the inspection is to uncover unexpected repair items or defects of some consequence and not to compile a list of minute flaws. Seeking absolute perfection is a needless and futile pursuit.

FIGURE 12-1 Exterior Inspection Report

EXTERIOR INSPECTION REPORT			
Name of Complex _____ No. of Units _____			
Address _____			
Component	Condition	Improvements	Est. Cost
Air Conditioning			
Boiler			
Building Walls			
Curbs and Gutters			
Elevators			
Fences			
Furnace			
Hot Water Heater			
Landscaping			
Laundry Room			
Mail Boxes			
Outdoor Lighting			
Parking Lot			
Pool			
Pool Filter			
Pool Heater			
Roof			
Sidewalks			
Steps			
Other			

FIGURE 12–2 Interior Inspection Report

INTERIOR INSPECTION REPORT			

Apartment Number _____ Unit Type _____

Component	Condition	Improvements	Est. Cost
GENERAL			
Carpets			
Ceilings			
Closets			
Doors			
Drapes			
Lights			
Walls			
Windows			
Other			
KITCHEN			
Cabinets			
Dishwasher			
Disposal			
Flooring			
Refrigerator			
Sink			
Stove			
Stove Hood			
BATHROOM			
Cabinets			
Exhaust Fan			
Faucets			
Flooring			
Shower			
Shower Door			
Sink			
Toilet			
Towel Racks			
Tub			

Notes _____

_____

_____

If there are maintenance items that need to be brought to the seller's attention for renegotiation, put the buyer's points in writing and take the list to the seller. When? You're right: *without delay*.

There will probably be some back-and-forth negotiations concerning what the seller will or will not do about correcting problems with the building or making a price adjustment. However, since the buyer's requests for adjustments are backed by the inspection reports and in some instances professional opinions, a motivated seller usually will be amenable to a reasonable compromise.

At this point you should have all of the buyer's contingencies satisfied with the exception of the contingency for obtaining new financing. In addition to inspecting the property, the buyer will have reviewed and approved the rental agreements, operating statements, inventory list and maintenance contracts. Assuming that any problems or discrepancies that may have surfaced in the process have been resolved, you are now ready to begin working on the buyer's loan commitment. The reason to wait until now to apply for financing is that the buyer will have to pay loan application and appraisal fees at this point. Therefore, you'll want to make sure that all other contingencies have been removed before the buyer incurs these expenses.

Decide with the buyer where to go for financing. This is when you'll be glad you spent some time earlier getting to know the most competitive, knowledgeable and helpful lenders in your area. Go to the selected lender, explain your buyer's needs and ask for the necessary loan applications. Then *hand-deliver* these financial forms to the buyer. See to it that he fills out the information quickly so that you can pick up the documents and return them *in person* to the lender.

Time is of the essence!

Have the lender give you an estimate of the time that will be required to process the loan application and fund the loan. Be prepared to ride herd on lenders during the approval process. If you don't keep track of how loan arrangements are coming along, things will tend to drag on. Therefore, make sure the lender adheres to the loan approval and funding date.

The lender will also want to schedule an appraisal of the apartment building. Make sure the lender works through *you* to arrange the appraiser's appointment to see the property. It is of paramount importance that you know what is happening at all times during the transaction so that you can keep things on track and going in the right direction throughout the entire chain of events. Make sure the buyer and seller are also completely informed for the status of the sale. Maintain their enthusiasm and interest by keeping both parties aware of the progress being made. Leaving your clients in the dark can leave you out in the cold. Miscommunication or lack of communication often sounds the death knell for many deals.

For some reason or other, *insurance* often is forgotten about until the last minute, and such a delay could put the whole transaction out of kilter. The lender, naturally, will not fund the loan until there is insurance protection for the money. Many lenders will want to see the actual insurance policy, not just a so-called binder to tide things over until the policy is written. Unfortunately, it may take from two to three weeks for an insurance company to issue a policy. By that time, you might need a whip and a chair to keep the buyer and seller under control! As soon as the buyer has applied for his loan, have him contact his insurance agent to begin preparing the insurance policy. Better yet, ask the buyer to let *you* contact the agent. Then, direct the insurance agent to speak with the loan officer to make sure the policy is written according to the coverages required by the lender.

You should also ask the buyer to determine whether he wants to retain the present resident manager or hire a new one. If the apartment building contains only a few units and a change is desired, the new owner could appoint one of the more reliable tenants as resident manager for a small monthly fee. Or he could advertise for a new manager if the apartment property is a large one. Personnel recruitment isn't exactly your responsibility, but the buyer will appreciate your interest in the matter. That makes for good client relations. Remember, your present buyer could refer other clients to you or he might call on you to help him purchase another apartment building in the future.

THE GRAND FINALE: CLOSING THE ESCROW

You're almost there. So let's get on with the fun part—the closing! When the loan officer informs you that the financing has been approved, ask him how long it will take the processing department to draft the buyer's loan papers. Typically this is a four- to ten-day period. Provided all other details are in order (and they should be), funding the loan and having the buyer deposit his or her down payment into escrow should be your last events before closing. Therefore, once you know when the loan will be ready to fund, schedule an escrow closing date. Verify it with the buyer, seller and escrow officer and hold to it! Think of that date as set in concrete. I want to make a strong point here because a delayed escrow can be a sale in trouble. Make sure that everyone sticks to that date—no matter what. Be determined to close escrow on that day even if you have to make it right under the wire. It's worth it, for *all* involved.

A day or two before the closing is to take place, you can provide an additional service to your buyer and seller. Contact the utility companies, maintenance contractors such as trash pickup, pool cleaning, landscaping care and other services and notify them of the impending sale date. These service suppliers can then take any necessary steps to transfer the contractual commitments to the buyer's name and prorate current charges to the date of closing. This is important. The seller, for instance, wouldn't be happy to learn that the utility bills were still being charged to him many days after escrow closed. You should also make arrangements with the seller to pick up any keys to the building and give them to the buyer once the transaction is complete.

On the day of closing, the escrow officer will make all necessary prorations, including rents and property taxes, and transfer all tenant deposits to the buyer. She will also prepare an escrow closing statement showing the charges and credits made to both buyer and seller.

And now, the envelope, please.

Hey, it has your name on it!

And will you look at that commission check!

Congratulations. You've earned it. Most important, you've earned your place as an apartment sales specialist. From now on, the only direction to go is up. The next chapter contains some final thoughts to help you reach those heights faster.

SUMMING UP WHAT YOU'VE LEARNED
IN CHAPTER 12

Closing the deal you've worked so hard to bring about depends on how you handle those all-important final steps in completing the transaction. Guide yourself by these important points.

    1. Arrange an on-site inspection of the apartment property as soon as the purchase offer is accepted.

    2. Be sure tenants are notified in advance of the inspection.

    3. Encourage the buyer to inspect *all* apartment interiors.

    4. Remove purchase contingencies as soon as possible.

    5. Carefully select an escrow officer experienced in *apartment* transactions. No one else will do.

    6. Coordinate financing arrangements between the buyer and the lender. Have the lender set a time schedule for loan approval.

    7. Don't forget the *insurance*. Writing a policy may take two or three weeks. Don't risk a last minute hang-up.

    8. Keep your buyer and seller informed about *all* details.

    9. Never mail transaction documents! You must hand-deliver all pertinent papers directly to the parties involved.

    10. Don't let *anything* delay the closing of escrow.

CHAPTER **13**

It's All Yours!

*"We should all be concerned with
the future, because we will spend
the rest of our lives there."*

—CHARLES KETTERING

You've come a long way since you started reading this book. In fact, you actually have a 12-year head start on knowing how to sell apartment buildings. That is literally true because it took me 12 years to develop the techniques I've passed along to you. You have not only saved a lot of time, but you have been spared the often-difficult experience of learning by trial and error.

I have tested and proven the methods I have taught you in this book hundreds of times, and I can assure you again that they *work*. By following the procedures I have described, no limits exist to the income and personal rewards you can achieve.

However, you'll need to take one more important step, which I can best illustrate with an experience I had a number of years ago.

When I was getting ready to make the South Pacific voyage I mentioned at the beginning of this book, I was tremendously busy with all the preparations. I studied charts and maps, read books, made lists of supplies, learned about the latest navigational equipment and did many other things. After all, I reasoned, a two-year cruise isn't something you just jump into. But to a certain extent, I was wrong.

Almost every time I went down to the slip where my boat was moored, I noticed an elderly man nearby, sitting on the dock and puffing away at his pipe. With his rugged face, toughened hands, weathered jacket and visored cap, he looked as if he had just stepped out of a Joseph Conrad novel about adventure on the high seas.

Whenever I arrived at my boat to stow away more supplies and check out the craft, the old salt watched me with flinty eyes that gleamed with a sparkle of humor. We used to greet each other and exchange a few words about the weather, boats and sailing.

It occurred to me that a long-experienced mariner such as this man could give me some valuable advice, so I asked him if there was anything in particular I should know about the journey I had planned.

"Well," the veteran seafarer said, "I seen a lotta' folks get ready to sail. Matter o' fact, some of 'em spend so much time gettin' ready, they never go." He tapped the ashes from his pipe and looked me straight in the eye. "They forget the most important thing about makin' a trip," he said.

"What's that?" I asked.

He replied, "Leavin' the dock."

He was right, and I can't think of better advice to give you.

You have read this book and now know the hows and whys of selling apartment buildings. You now possess the basic knowledge you need to succeed. But knowledge alone won't put money into your bank account. What you need at this point is experience and the only way to get it is to start right in. So it's time for you to leave the dock and set sail into your new and exciting future.

Think of this book as a map to chart the course for your career. Refer to it often and follow every step exactly as I have described it. Soon, you'll be putting your own personal touches to the techniques I have taught you. And that's the way it should be. This is *your* career, and the more you put your own personality imprint on your sales methods, the sooner you'll succeed.

Keep in mind these few final pointers to help guide you along the way.

1. *Always put the client first*—ahead of making the sale and earning a commission check. In all the years I've been in this business, I've never made an enemy of a client. And there isn't a single past client who wouldn't invite me over for dinner. I don't have a magical charm that casts a spell over people. I simply put the client's interests above my own. Granted, sometimes you may have to count to ten to keep your patience with some people, but make that extra effort. Believe me, *it pays*.

Remember that you are embarking on a long-term career, not simply trying to make a few quick sales here and there. When you do your job right, you won't have to worry about commissions. With honesty and dedication they'll surely come your way.

2. *Never, never do anything to jeopardize your client's position.* Promise only what you can deliver, keep your word in all matters and help your client in every way you can. Satisfied clients are your best spokespeople, and you cannot afford to lose goodwill.

3. *Keep expanding your knowledge.* Those who think they have all the answers usually have the wrong ones. Ask questions. Try new approaches with buyers and sellers. Talk to other brokers. Stay updated on market conditions in your area. Make each transaction a learning experience for the next one.

Learning is a constant process. In my years of experience, having sold millions of dollars worth of apartment properties, I still keep discovering new ideas to help me sell, as well as finding better ways to use time-tested methods.

4. *Recognize your own value.* You now know more about selling apartment buildings than most of your friends and business associates. Therefore, you *are* an apartment sales specialist. Your personality can be your greatest asset. Each of us has certain qualities that make us unique. Use your specific qualities to good advantage. Be yourself and you'll always be at your best.

5. *Be bold and confident about making sales.* When I use the word *bold*, I am not suggesting that you be pushy and overly aggressive. Rather, I urge you *always* to take the lead in dealing with buyers and sellers. Keep things moving. Most people genuinely appreciate being guided intelligently and helpfully in their decisions. By nudging and persuading your clients to complete a sound transaction, you are actually doing them a favor. Even if the owner wants to sell and the buyer wants to purchase a certain building, inertia alone often brings things to a creeping pace or even to a halt. You can energize both parties by pressing for a sale. If you don't take action in a slow-motion situation, no one else will.

6. *Above all, be professional.* The highest compliment you can receive is to have a buyer or seller tell others that you are a real pro who knows how to put deals together.

7. *Visualize your success.* Picture yourself creating a sale and receiving a large commission check. See yourself depositing the

check. Create a mental scene in which you are enjoying the kind of rich rewarding life you desire. Your subconscious mind is a vast reservoir of personal power and the more positive images you plant in your subconscious, the sooner your dreams will materialize. And this is not merely conjecture. It's a basic truth about making genuine progress in life. You will become what you truly believe about yourself. And that belief can be totally positive because you have so much to be confident about.

Everything you've ever wanted—a high income, a fine home, financial independence and freedom to do the things you enjoy—the best imaginable future is waiting for you.

My best wishes for the success I know you can achieve. It's all yours!

INDEX